BI

| 100 ESSENTIAL CDs | THE ROUGH GUIDE |

There are more than one hundred and fifty Rough Guide
travel, phrasebook, and music titles, covering destinations
from Amsterdam to Zimbabwe, languages from Czech to
Vietnamese, and musics from World to Opera and Jazz

Other 100 Essential CD titles

Classical • Country • Opera
Reggae • Rock • Soul • World

Rough Guides on the Internet

www.roughguides.com

Rough Guide Credits

Text editor: Joe Staines
Series editor: Mark Ellingham
Typesetting: Robert Evers

Publishing Information

This first edition published October 2000 by
Rough Guides Ltd, 62–70 Shorts Gardens, London WC2H 9AB

Distributed by the Penguin Group:

Penguin Books Ltd, 27 Wrights Lane, London W8 5TZ
Penguin Putnam, Inc. 375 Hudson Street, New York 10014, USA
Penguin Books Australia Ltd, 487 Maroondah Highway,
PO Box 257, Ringwood, Victoria 3134, Australia
Penguin Books Canada Ltd, 10 Alcorn Avenue,
Toronto, Ontario, Canada M4V 1E4
Penguin Books (NZ) Ltd, 182–190 Wairau Road,
Auckland 10, New Zealand

Typeset in Bembo and Helvetica to an original design by Henry Iles.
Printed in Spain by Graphy Cems.

© Greg Ward, 208pp

A catalogue record for this book is available from the British Library.
ISBN 1-85828-560-7

Blues

100 ESSENTIAL CDs THE ROUGH GUIDE

by Greg Ward

ROUGH
GUIDES

Contents List

Introduction

The Rough Guide to Essential Blues CDs celebrates the first century of the blues by selecting a hundred of the finest blues CDs currently available. Some are little-known historical documents, others have sold in their millions; together, they tell a fascinating story of the music's development, but all are included, first and foremost, because they make fabulous listening.

As folk wisdom almost has it, writing about the blues is like whistling about chickens. Even defining the blues is all but impossible. No one knows where it came from; it just seemed to emerge fully fledged, a hundred years ago, among black Americans of the so-called Deep South. While elements of the music can be traced back to West Africa, bottleneck guitar seems to have originated in Hawaii, and many early "blues" songs were actually written for the vaudeville stage. Nonetheless, the blues has remained strongly identified with the South; almost all of the artists included here were born somewhere between East Texas and Georgia, even if they eventually found fame in the cities of the North.

The best-known version of blues history concentrates on the pre-World War II "Delta blues" of Mississippi, as played on acoustic instruments by artists like Son House and Robert Johnson. This was adapted from the late 1940s onwards by Mississippian migrants to Chicago, notably Muddy Waters and Howlin' Wolf, to create the urban blues. That majestic tradition forms the core of this book, but newcomers to the music will find much more besides, including the lighter, more technically accomplished guitar-picking styles of Georgia and the Carolinas.

In the early days, record companies used the label "blues" as a catch-all description for a very broad spectrum of black popular music, but in the last fifty years the definition has narrowed as the blues has proved to be the bedrock from which genres such as rock'n'roll, R&B, soul and even rock have split away. I have, therefore excluded those artists – such as Little Richard, Ray

Charles, Aretha Franklin and Jimi Hendrix – who started in the blues but moved on before producing their greatest work.

Thanks to still-creative veterans like John Lee Hooker and R.L. Burnside, as well as newcomers like Corey Harris and Alvin Hart, the blues is maintaining its capacity to delight and surprise now that it has entered the twenty-first century. Inevitably, however, there's an emphasis here on the seminal recordings of the 1920s and 1930s. Devotees of more recent artists may spot what they regard as glaring omissions; deciding how to make room for them is a much harder task, and I still regret having to restrict such major figures as Howlin' Wolf to just one album.

Acknowledgements

Anyone writing about the blues owes an immense debt to researchers such as Gayle Wardlow and Stephen Calt, who rescued not only the life stories of many blues artists but, in some instances, the actual recordings themselves. In addition, the works of Paul Oliver, Peter Guralnick and Charles Shaar Murray contributed joy and inspiration to the writing of this book.

I'd also like to thank Bob Sulatycki for introducing me to the treasures of his brother's record collection 25 years ago, and my own brother Julian for generously sharing his books and records with me. At home, Samantha Cook has as ever been both an inspiration and an invaluable source of strength and confidence, while Rob Humphreys, Rob Jones, Jules Brown and Julia Vellacott have all provided vital moral support.

At Rough Guides, I'd like to thank Joe Staines and Jonathan Buckley for their committed editing, Robert Evers for his conscientious typesetting, as well as all the authors of the other "100 Essential CD" guides – especially Al "Rock" Spicer – for their encouragement and help.

Greg Ward

Kokomo Arnold

Old Original Kokomo Blues

Catfish, 1999; recorded 1934–38

James "Kokomo" Arnold fits few of the standard stereotypes of blues legend. Though you'd expect such a gifted slide guitarist to come from Mississippi, he was in fact born in Georgia, and modelled his technique as much on Hawaiian music as on the Delta blues. In being equally adept at the fast finger-picking styles of the East Coast, he represented a synthesis of traditions usually thought of as entirely distinct. What's more, despite cutting some of the most acclaimed classics of the early "country" blues, he made his living not from raising hogs or growing cotton in the South but as a bootlegger in Prohibition-era Chicago. He even told an interviewer that "I was never interested in making records, and I always preferred to live a quiet life; just unknown in my basement." Thus he told his landlady to say he was out when they came to fetch him for a Decca session in the mid-1930s; stopped recording altogether in 1938; and declined to come out of retirement when he was "rediscovered" during the folk boom of the 1960s.

Kokomo Arnold recorded a couple of barely noticed discs in Memphis in 1930, under the name of "Gitfiddle Jim". Catfish's compilation **Old Original Kokomo Blues** picks up the story with his return to the studio in Chicago four years later. This time around, his debut release for Decca had an immediate impact. Old Original Kokomo Blues itself was named after a brand of coffee, and loosely adapted from Scrapper Blackwell's "Kokomo Blues". Both in its tune, and in lyrics like "baby don't you want to go" and "one and one is two, two and two is four", it was clearly the prototype for Robert Johnson's "Sweet Home Chicago". The other side, Milkcow Blues, was promoted by Decca with the slogan, "it's the greatest record ever made"; it was to receive the unique accolade of being covered by both Robert Johnson and Elvis Presley.

The most instantly impressive aspect of Arnold's music is the blistering speed of his fingers. On faster numbers like The Twelves (Dirty Dozen) and Policy Wheel Blues, he'd lay his guitar on his lap, picking with his left hand and manipulating the slide with his right. He was soon in demand for sessions with other artists, such as pianists Roosevelt Sykes (whose signature tune The Honeydripper is included here) and Peetie Wheatstraw (as on Mister Charlie).

Arnold was also a fine singer, whether using his customary slightly quavery falsetto or in the deeper voice he used for his lovely version of Leroy Carr's How Long, How Long Blues. He brought an easy facility to attractive novelty songs like Paddlin' Madeline Blues and Salty Dog, and a more know-ing air to hokum material such as You Should Not A' Done It and the frankly misogynistic Cause You're Dirty. On the other hand, there's seldom any sense of personal passion in his singing and he always remains the professional entertainer rather than the tortured poet. Though he's credited as having written all except one of these 23 tracks, you'd also have to suspect that most were in the public domain. Still, in the history of slide gui-tar he's unquestionably at the top of the family tree; after all, Sagefield Woman Blues features the first known use of the phrase "I believe I'll dust my broom", while the actual song "Dust My Broom", as recorded by Robert Johnson and Elmore James, got its tune from Sissyman Blues.

Kokomo Arnold was working in a Chicago steel mill when the record companies finally came knocking at his door again. Though he made a few club appearances before his death in 1968, he consistently refused to re-enter the studios.

➲ We almost chose **Complete Recorded Works Vol.1**, Document, 1994

Blind Blake

Ragtime Guitar's Foremost Fingerpicker

Yazoo, 1990; recorded 1926–31

Although Blind Blake is invariably recognized as a pioneer of the blues – during his heyday, only Blind Lemon Jefferson sold more records in the "race market" – his music doesn't lend itself to easy categorization. In almost a hundred sides cut for Paramount Records, his repertoire ranged across vaudeville, popular dance formats like the Charleston, early jazz and boogie, as well as the ragtime that provides the title for the best single-volume collection of his work, **Ragtime Guitar's Foremost Fingerpicker**. Only nine of the 23 tracks here (not necessarily among the thirteen whose names include the word "blues") are twelve-bar blues. What they all have in common, however, is the expertise of Blind Blake's self-taught instrumental technique.

For such a prolific artist, amazingly little is known about the man himself. Blind from birth, he's thought to have come from either northern Florida or southern Georgia, and to have been in his mid- to late thirties by the time of his first Paramount session in Chicago in 1926. Over the next six years the company released roughly a disc a month, without beginning to exhaust the wealth of material he'd accumulated travelling with medicine shows and vaudeville troupes. That songbook alone would make Blind Blake a seminal figure, but he's not primarily what blues historians call a "songster". What continues to impress listeners today is what awed Big Bill Broonzy when he first ran into Blake into Chicago: "He made [his guitar] sound like every instrument in the band – saxophone, trombone, clarinets, bass fiddles, drums – everything. I never had seed then and I haven't to this day yet seed no one that could take his natural fingers and pick as much guitar as Blind Blake."

Paramount boasted in their advertisements of Blake's "famous piano-sounding guitar", heard at its finest on instrumental sides such as Seaboard Blues, on which he sounds like a veritable one-man band, and the appealing Blind Arthur's Breakdown ("breakdown" being a dance not a mental collapse). That the latter was credited on its original release to "Blind Arthur", incidentally, is taken as evidence that his real name was Arthur Blake. Similarly, the familiarity with the Gullah dialect displayed on Southern Rag suggests that he came from the Georgia Sea Islands.

While Blake regularly accompanied blues artists like Ma Rainey, he also recorded intriguing collaborations with artists from outside the genre. On Hastings Street he enthusiastically keeps pace with the boogie-woogie piano of Detroit's Charlie Spand, while C.C. Pill Blues finds him teamed with the jazz clarinet of Johnny Dodds and the eerie slide whistle of Jimmy Bertrand. Police Dog Blues demonstrates, on the other hand, that despite his often inexpressive voice he could deliver an emotive blues performance with the best of them. His skills as a pure entertainer are at their most apparent on novelty pieces like Skeedle Loo Doo Blues and Diddie Wa Diddie.

Blake's career came to an abrupt end as a result of the Depression in 1932. After the unlikeliest of swansongs, "Champagne Charlie Is My Name", he simply disappeared. According to Big Bill Broonzy, he died shortly afterwards, when he fell over in a blizzard and, "him being so fat", couldn't get up again – though that hardly jibes with the elegant figure in his only photo. Others suggest that he was knocked down by a streetcar in Atlanta in 1941. He's sometimes said to have inspired the subsequent emergence of an "East Coast" school of blues musicians – and you can certainly hear Reverend Gary Davis presaged in the lovely You Gonna Quit Me Blues – but his greatest legacy is his own recorded work, and Yazoo have done him proud.

➲ We almost chose **Complete Recorded Works Vol.1**, Document, 1994

Bobby Bland

The Voice

Ace, 1991; recorded 1959–69

Bobby Bland may not play an instrument or write his own material but he's spent fifty years at the forefront of the blues pantheon thanks to his rich, irresistible gospel-drenched voice. **The Voice** collects 26 examples of Bland in his absolute prime, pouring his heart out for Duke Records atop the magnificent brass arrangements of Joe Scott. Reaching beyond the confines of the blues, Bland and Scott established the template for what became soul music. If Bland had only managed to extend his run in the pop charts beyond the early 1960s, he might now be remembered as the greatest soul singer of all time; instead, almost all of the millions he did sell were to older black audiences, and he has remained forever identified with the blues.

Robert Calvin Bland was born just outside Memphis in 1930. Moving into the city in 1947, he hooked up with fellow aspiring musicians such as B.B. King, Junior Parker and Johnny Ace as the Beale Streeters, and cut his first discs for Sun in the early 1950s. Thanks to Parker, he signed with local label Duke Records shortly before being drafted into the army in 1952. When he returned in 1955, Duke had been sold to Houston businessman Don Robey and it was in Texas, as Bobby "Blue" Bland, that he finally carved out his own identity.

In a sense, Bland's voice was not so much *his* instrument as Joe Scott's. As musical director at Duke, Scott crafted every detail of the formula that brought Bland fame. Unlike the many gospel-trained singers who have gravitated towards the blues, Bland moved in the opposite direction, grafting gospel techniques onto his previous Roy Brown-influenced "blues shouting" style. Thus the trademark throaty gargle he called his "squall" came from the Reverend C.L. Franklin, Aretha's father, and first appeared on his 1958 classic "Little Boy Blue".

Gospel music may be characterized by spontaneous outbursts of feeling, but there was nothing improvised about Bland on record or even on stage. Scott persuaded him to slow down, and remodelled his phrasing on Nat "King" Cole and Bland's own idol, Perry Como. Whatever the songwriting credits say – most belong either to Robey or to his pseudonym "Deadric Malone" – Scott also wrote the bulk of the songs, tailoring them to Bobby's strengths. As Bland put it, "I would say he was everything."

It's impossible to do justice here to more than a few of the gems on *The Voice*, but Bland's definitive cut of T-Bone Walker's Stormy Monday Blues has to be acknowledged. Bland's breathy, half-whispered vocals are matched throughout by Wayne Bennett's delicate, flowing guitar, which deftly changes the pace as both build to an impassioned climax. The brassy Turn On Your Lovelight, by contrast, rocks from the very start, though Bland remains gloriously composed as the drums and horns go wild behind him. A different trick is played out on Ain't Nothing You Can Do – Bland's final pop hit from 1964 – when, despite his original careful precision, he's drawn into a frenzied battle against the relentlessly mounting blasts from the brass section.

Everything Bland and Scott touched seemed to turn to gold, whether it was the campy cod rumba of Sometimes You Got To Cry A Little and Blue Moon, the out-and-out gospel of Yield Not To Temptation, or the sugar-soft soul of Shoes. As the decade went by, perhaps Bland was trying a little too hard to emulate the mainstream success of Sam Cooke, as on Ask Me 'Bout Nothing (But The Blues), or Otis Redding (Back In The Same Old Bag Again), but God only knows he deserved it.

➲ We almost chose **I Pity The Fool, The Duke Recordings**, MCA, 1992

Bobby Bland

His California Album

Beat Goes On, 1998; recorded 1973

By the 1970s, Bobby Bland was something of an anachronism. Not only had he failed to achieve success with white audiences, but he seemed too closely associated with what younger blacks saw as the stuck-in-the-past self-pity of the blues to reinvent himself as a self-affirming soul man. In truth, he'd never shown much personal confidence, continuing to work as Junior Parker's valet, driver and warm-up man, for example, long after he'd made his own string of hits. Now, an acrimonious split with longtime arranger Joe Scott in 1968 had put an end not only to the stream of almost forty R&B smashes he'd recorded for Duke in just ten years, but also to his lucrative semi-permanent life on the road.

The sale of Duke Records to ABC in 1973 kick-started a new phase in Bland's career. The very title of his first ABC release, **His California Album**, appeared to proclaim it as a dream come true for both Bland and his public. California was so much the epicentre of the "hip" recording industry – so the implication ran – that it was a privilege for a blues singer to record there, and a guarantee of success. The irony, of course, is that Bland's previous work for Duke (see p.5) still stands as consummately inventive music, and it's the "contemporary adult rock" sound of California that has dated.

Nonetheless, despite the disdain of many blues critics, *His California Album* remains eminently worthwhile. Although in retreating from the brass-heavy Duke sound Bland was to some extent turning his back on the soul style he'd helped to create, his voice was as soulful as ever. Too soulful for his own good, really. With his much-professed fondness for crooners like Perry Como, he'd probably have loved to become a pop crooner himself; but every time he opened his mouth, the emotion just cascaded out.

Produced by Steve Barri, and arranged by Michael Omartian, the backing on *His California Album* was competent rather than inspired. There's a funky resonance to the bass, and a penetrating edge to the guitars, but it all remains tastefully deferent to Bland's singing rather than sparring against it, and forever liable to be swamped by syrupy strings. But from the moment Bland unleashes his "squall" on opening track This Time I'm Gone For Good, his ability to transcend the setting is clear.

The real showstopper is the five-minute cut of Goin' Down Slow, a ballad by "St Louis Jimmy" Oden that's perfectly attuned to the morbid fascination Bland had once displayed on "St James Infirmary". Where Howlin' Wolf roared his way through this tale of a high roller anticipating his own death, Bland takes things very slowly, milking every last bittersweet drop. Omartian's restrained piano leads the funeral procession, joined by a new element with each passing verse.

Even though Duke was now defunct, Don Robey managed to claim credit for four tracks. Elsewhere, (If Loving You Is Wrong) I Don't Want To Be Right – a product of the Stax stable that had been a massive hit in 1972 for Luther Ingram – sees Bland take on the persona of the adulterous older male. That territory became a mainstay of his subsequent career, and was even more fruitfully explored by Z.Z. Hill. Other covers included Gladys Knight And The Pips' I've Got To Use My Imagination, and Leon Russell's Help Me Through The Day. Both *His California Album* and follow-up *Dreamer* sold well enough with rock audiences to rekindle interest in the Duke era as well, while Bland himself is still going strong to this day, with ten Malaco albums since 1985 and frequent concert tours.

➲ We almost chose **Dreamer**, MCA, 1991

James Booker

Resurrection Of The Bayou Maharajah

Rounder, 1998; recorded 1977–82

The fact that James Booker could and did play absolutely anything on the piano, using sheer intuition to string together bizarre medleys drawn from the most disparate sources and genres, makes it hard to argue a case for him as a blues artist per se. The alternative – that he might slip through the net, and you might go through life never hearing **Resurrection Of The Bayou Maharajah** – doesn't bear thinking about. Culled from his solo gigs at New Orleans' Maple Leaf Bar between 1977 and 1982, the album is a seventy-minute cornucopia of electrifying keyboard genius, the excitement of which never palls.

Booker himself was a troubled man, whose sorry saga of mental illness, drug addiction and incarceration ended with his premature death at the age of 43 in 1983. Born the son of a preacherman in December 1939, he was a child star in New Orleans by 1953, when Booker Boy and the Rhythmaires recorded Dave Bartholomew's "Doing the Hambone". He spent the next twenty years touring with Earl King, B.B. King and Joe Tex, and playing alongside Junior Parker and Bobby Bland in Houston for Peacock Records, for whom he had his own hit, "Gonzo", in 1960. Stories at the time tell of him evading drug busts, talking his way out of courts or police stations, or simply freaking out and disappearing. According to Dr John, he lost his left eye – thus necessitating his trademark black eyepatch complete with silver star – when he was attacked by a bodyguard as he attempted to get paid again for a job for which he'd already cashed three cheques. Dr John also recalls that, as a member of his band in the 1970s, Booker "just overran me, left me in the dirt."

It was this unreliability that, in the end, forced Booker to work solo, but his weekly Maple Leaf gigs were unpredictable affairs, in which he might barely play a note, let alone an entire song. On his good days, however, he absolutely soared. Five of the eleven tracks here are extended medleys, in which he exuberantly reveals connections at first apparent only to himself, as rhythms – all but obscured beneath his ebullient improvisations and introspective interludes – suddenly erupt to the surface. From the yelp that introduces Slow Down to the dying notes of Irene Goodnight an hour later, you never know where his musical imagination may lead. Stops along the way include soul anthems like Knock On Wood and a barely recognizable I Heard It Through The Grapevine; New Orleans stompers such as Lawdy Miss Clawdy and All By Myself; out-and-out blues like St James Infirmary; and even, as befits the self-proclaimed "Black Liberace", a dash of Chopin's Minute Waltz.

For all the mind-boggling flurries and flying New Orleans triplets coming from the upper reaches of the keyboard, the experience is rooted in Booker's uncanny, unfailing sense of rhythm. As he said himself, "There is nothing I don't like about rhythm and blues . . . the rhythm makes you dance and the blues make you think." Everything gels into place during the awesome Papa Was A Rascal, an autobiographical masterpiece that's half lament, half manifesto: "You know my papa was a preacher, and a lover too. Well if my papa was a rascal, why can't I be one too?". Despite the odd snatch of "Flight Of The Bumblebee" and admonition that "we all got to watch out for the CIA", it's a perfectly paced, dynamic performance that leaves you wishing Booker had found the time to make more than just two studio albums in his lifetime.

➲ We almost chose **Classified**, Rounder, 1998

Big Bill Broonzy

Where The Blues Began

Recall, 2000; recorded 1928–46

Much like Leadbelly before him, Big Bill Broonzy turned himself into such a legend during the final years before his death in 1958 that he allowed his own genuine talents and achievements to become obscured. As both guitarist and songwriter, he ranked among the very best to emerge during the first great flowering of the blues. A master of early guitar-picking in such blues-related genres as rag and hokum, he swiftly moved on to record sophisticated jazz-imbued small-group numbers that became the major prototype for Chicago's subsequent urban blues boom. After World War II, however, he deliberately turned the clock back, donning overalls to perform solo as "the last of the blues singers." While his Everyman schtick – "I guess all songs is folk songs – I never heard no horse sing 'em" – brought him huge success in Europe, in particular, it did long-lasting damage to his reputation as an innovator. Squeezing forty tracks on two CDs, Recall's cut-price **Where The Blues Began** compilation sets out to redress the balance, with a superb cross-section of cuts from Broonzy's most productive years.

Big Bill was born in Mississippi in 1893, and was raised in Arkansas from the age of 8. He was inspired to make his first instrument, a fiddle, by an itinerant musician who was known as See See Rider in honour of his favourite song. Torn at first between the church and the blues, he was soon performing for white audiences across Arkansas, Mississippi and Texas. When military service in France during World War I opened his eyes to the fact that "you never be called a man in the South", he struck out for Chicago in 1920. Encounters there with the likes of Papa Charlie Jackson and Blind Blake led to his taking up the guitar, and ultimately to a debut session for Paramount in 1927. The following year, his theme song, Big Bill Blues, notched up his first significant sales.

Broonzy's ability to stand alone as a guitarist is amply demonstrated by his superlative flat-picking on How You Want It Done?, and his precise delivery of Worrying You Off My Mind, a variation on the "Sitting On Top Of The World" theme. Whether recording under his own name, however, or backing someone else, he loved to work with other musicians. Early cohorts included banjoist Steel Smith, as on Too Too Train Blues, and the pianist Georgia Tom Dorsey. By the mid-1930s, he was regularly recording alongside groups that typically comprised piano, bass and drums. Often there'd be a clarinet or fiddle to take the solos as well, as on his version of C.C. Rider.

In 1938, Broonzy presented himself on the New York stage, at John Hammond's epochal Spirituals to Swing concert, as the archetypal backwoods bluesman. Back home in Chicago, on the other hand, he had already embarked on his most prolific period as songwriter and recording star, writing an astonishing succession of future standards. Working for the Bluebird label with sidemen such as Memphis Slim on piano, Sonny Boy Williamson I on harp, and Washboard Sam, he reeled off songs like Key To The Highway, Wee Wee Hours, All By Myself and I Feel So Good. Though in other hands they were to become blues and even rock'n'roll classics, all are better described as amplified than electrified.

Even when working with a fully fledged R&B band in 1945 and 1946, shouting over the saxes on numbers like Partnership Woman and Stop Lying Woman, Broonzy never showed much interest in testing the limits of his electric guitar. Later on, as his protégé Muddy Waters stepped to the fore, Broonzy contented himself instead with playing up to his persona as "Big Bill".

⮑ We almost chose **The Young Big Bill Broonzy**, Yazoo, 1991

Clarence "Gatemouth" Brown

Texas Swing

Rounder, 1998; recorded 1981–82

Despite his repeated insistence that "I hate for people to refer to me as a blues musician", Clarence "Gatemouth" Brown has produced at least one essential blues album in each of the last six decades. True, his range extends so far as to make him virtually unclassifiable, but his multi-instrumental flair has consistently enriched the blues ever since he grabbed T-Bone Walker's guitar and burst onto the stage of Houston's Bronze Peacock club in 1947. With its exuberant cross-genre sweep, **Texas Swing**, an hour-long collection of Brown's finest work of the 1980s, makes a fabulous introduction to one of American music's greatest originals.

Born in Vinton, Louisiana, in April 1924, and raised just across the border in Orange, Texas, Clarence Brown was cast in the mould of his father, who played zydeco and hillbilly music on both fiddle and accordion, singing in (Cajun) French or English as the mood took him. Nicknamed "Gatemouth" on account of his booming voice, he started out as a drummer, but first drew significant attention as a guitarist. Impressed by Brown's fluid, jazz-tinged guitar style – not to mention his flamboyant dress sense and stage presence – Don Robey, the owner of the Bronze Peacock, moved swiftly to become his manager. A contract with Atlantic produced disappointing results, so Robey set up Peacock Records in 1948 to record Brown himself. That association lasted until 1961, with Brown producing a stream of searing, guitar-based, horn-rich R&B classics that were sadly more influential than they were commercially successful.

The next twenty years saw Gatemouth exploring country and roots music, and touring extensively in Europe and Africa as well as within the United States. In 1981, tapes made for Real Records in Bogalusa, Louisiana, were picked up by Rounder Records and released as the Grammy award-winning *Alright Again!*. *Texas Swing* includes eight tracks from that album, plus nine more from its 1982 follow-up, *One More Mile*. The compilation's strength lies in the cumulative impact of Brown's breathtaking skill on both guitar and violin, framed by imaginative and intelligent horn arrangements.

Brown always likes to take things one stage further. As he puts it, "I don't like just coming out with the same crap as everybody else." Thus he'll use his guitar to play phrases you'd expect to hear from the horns, or his violin to mimic human speech, while each horn in turn is individually "voiced". High spots as a guitarist come with his dazzlingly supple fretwork on his mentor T-Bone Walker's Strollin' With Bones, and his pupil Albert Collins' Frosty. Both Near Baku and Song For Renee are self-penned violin showcases, while ballads such as wartime chart-topper I Wonder, complete with pedal steel guitar, and his own Sometimes I Slip, adorned by a measured, lyrical tenor sax solo from Alvin "Red" Tyler, are sung with a rich, warm relish that sits oddly with his claim to hate singing. Perhaps the most enjoyable moments of all are the finger-snapping big-band blasts of Baby Take It Easy and Ain't That Dandy, on which Gatemouth proves he's equally capable of overshadowing the entire ensemble on either violin or guitar.

Adamantly refusing to be pigeonholed, forthrightly insisting that he won't play "that depressing Mississippi stuff" and "cannot stand that New Orleans type music", Gatemouth Brown may be too big for the blues, but the blues needs more like him. With the current swing revival, he's in his element, and is gleefully entering the 21st century at the helm of a bigger band than ever, even if his ever-restless mind can't help toying with the idea that trying out bluegrass instead might be kind of fun, too.

➲ We almost chose **The Original Peacock Recordings**, Rounder, 1990

R.L. Burnside

Come On In

Fat Possum, 1998

The most raucous, stimulating new blues being created at the end of the twentieth century was the work of a 73-year-old grandfather from Mississippi. **Come On In**, R.L. Burnside's 1998 album for the "post-punk" blues label Fat Possum, is a celebration of raw, barely controlled noise that would surely have delighted the pioneers of electric blues. True, Burnside's are not the only talents involved. The input of hip-hop-influenced producers Tom Rothrock and Alec Empire has incensed certain blues purists enough for them to send death threats to Fat Possum. But the result of the collaboration makes exhilarating sense when you actually listen to it. Burnside's music is rooted in the Mississippi hill country, not the Delta, and that's a tradition that depends on the long, drawn-out and deeply rhythmic reiteration of fragments and phrases. If hypnotic repetition is the target you're aiming for, then using tape loops makes a pretty effective short cut.

For most of his life, R.L. Burnside has been a farmer and a fisherman. He did record a couple of albums for Arhoolie in the 1960s, very much in the spirit of his hill-country mentor Mississippi Fred McDowell, but only in recent years has his reputation spread beyond his home town of Holly Springs. He developed his electrified sound through marathon gigs at close neighbour Junior Kimbrough's juke joint, backed by various permutations of his thirteen children and 22 grandchildren. Critic Robert Palmer first championed him in his film *Deep Blues*, and then produced his breakthrough Fat Possum album *Too Bad Jim* in 1994.

Burnside's unedited tapes were turned into *Come On In* without his active participation, and he's been quoted as saying "the first time I heard it, I said 'I don't know'." Nonetheless, for all its dub-style deconstructions, its ear-catching echoes and industrial-strength thuds, the characteristic building blocks of his blues are always apparent. The inclusion of a couple of solo tracks makes it clear that he needs no outside help to create an upliftingly almighty racket with his guitar.

While the individual songs on *Come On In* may not develop – in the finest hill-country tradition, they're not so much songs as aural collages – the album itself has a strong sense of direction. Opener Been Mistreated is a one-minute template for what's to come, its one line "Been mistreated and I don't mind dyin'" being repeated ten times over a steady drum pattern interspersed by a brief piercing guitar break. After a live solo rendition of Come On In, the simple riff of Let My Baby Ride ups the volume and then kicks in even louder. Individual instruments and Burnside's voice take turns to come to the fore as the rest drop out of the mix, but the relentless drive never lets up. An unlikely hit on MTV, the track is derived from "Snake Charmer" on the 1997 album *Mr Wizard*, while the ensuing It's Bad You Know draws its refrain from "Fireman Ring The Bell" on *Too Bad Jim*.

From there on, *Come On In* rings endless enjoyable changes on much the same material, including two remixes of the title track and two standout pieces on which production and programming is credited to Beal Dabbs. Don't Stop Honey is the shimmering distorted child of the ancient standard "Shake 'Em On Down", while Shuck Dub imbues "Let My Baby Ride" with a compellingly weird bass drone. Proceedings draw to a close with the apocalyptic thrash of Heat, in which R.L. can just about be heard joking about the sexual difficulties of getting old, while grandson Cedric Burnside flails exuberantly at his drum kit.

➲ We almost chose **Too Bad Jim**, Fat Possum, 1997

Cannon's Jug Stompers

The Complete Works

Yazoo, 1991; recorded 1928–30

Gus Cannon was a one-man history of Memphis music. Though he lived long enough to cut an album for Stax Records, he was already well into middle age when he first made it big. He was so old, in fact, that the blues hadn't even been invented when he learned to play the fiddle and banjo. In later life, he recalled performing into a primitive recording device in the Mississippi Delta in 1901. Had the resultant cylinder survived, he might now be hailed as the first bluesman of all; as it is, his fame rests on a three-year recording career at the end of the 1920s, and in particular his classic sides with Cannon's Jug Stompers. Their **Complete Works** make delightful listening. Even at the time, they sounded antiquated, but in their harmonica sound in particular they also presaged the future development of the blues.

Born in Red Banks, Mississippi, in 1883, Cannon once remarked that "they started to raise me in Mississippi, but the rope broke." Determined to make his living from music, he made his first banjo from a guitar neck stuck to a bread pan. After buying a real one, he taught himself to play it with a knife or bottleneck in the latest (Hawaiian-influenced) style, though on record he always stuck to a strongly percussive picking technique. Around 1910, at a lumber camp in Ripley, Tennessee, he teamed up with Noah Lewis, a harmonica wizard who "could play two harps at the same time, through his mouth and nose." Together with teenage guitarist Ashley Thompson, they performed for whoever would pay them, and made their first forays down to Beale Street in Memphis.

Cannon spent fifteen summers playing the banjo with touring medicine shows, before Paramount invited him to cut half a dozen discs in Chicago in 1927 as "Banjo Joe", alongside ragtime guitarist Blind Blake. Three months later, in the wake of their recent success with the Memphis Jug Band, the Victor company suggested Cannon put together his own jug band. He headed straight back to Ripley to find his former cohorts, and Cannon's Jug Stompers were born.

The basic concept of the jug band, in which one or more members blew across open clay jugs to create bass melodies and simple rhythms, emerged in Kentucky around 1915. With the Stompers, the "jug" element was relatively minor; Gus had both a metal kerosene can and a kazoo fixed to a rack in front of his face, which left his hands free for the banjo. The crucial element was Noah Lewis, who played the harp with extraordinary fluency. His work on instrumentals such as Noah's Blues was magnificent, and he also had his own stock of songs, such as Viola Lee Blues, later covered by The Grateful Dead, and the haunting World War I anthem Going To Germany.

Much of Cannon's own repertoire – like Feather Bed, which ruefully spoke of black expectations before and after the Civil War, and the rags-to-riches fantasy Money Never Runs Out, published in 1900 – dated back even further. Madison Street Rag, a ragtime piece with similarities to Charlie Patton's "Shake It And Break It", now sounds like the kind of "talking blues" Bob Dylan used to perform. The Stompers' best-known track, written by Cannon himself, comes from their final session. Walk Right In was originally a novelty dance number, but the Rooftop Singers' solemn folk remake in 1963 hit #1 in the pop charts, triggering a brief jug-band revival and a welcome dribble of royalties for Cannon. He lived on until 1979.

⮑ We almost chose **Walk Right In**, Stax, 1999

Captain Beefheart

Safe As Milk

Buddha, 1999; recorded 1967

If your only previous exposure to Captain Beefheart has been the interminable *Trout Mask Replica* – which regularly appears in top-hundred-album polls, even though there can be few people on the planet who have listened to it in its entirety – being told you've got to listen to **Safe As Milk** as well may come as bad news. And yet, of all the countless 1960s rock musicians who drew their primary influence from the blues, Captain Beefheart did the most interesting things with it and for sheer inventiveness his work outclasses all contemporary dabblings with so-called "blues rock".

The future Beefheart grew up as Don Vliet in Glendale, California, and teamed up with schoolfriend Frank Zappa in the late 1950s. At Zappa's suggestion, he named himself after the superhero of a never-made movie, *Captain Beefheart vs The Grunt People*. His first "Magic Band" were picked up by A&M Records in 1965, following an appearance at the Hollywood Teen Fair, and then promptly dropped after two singles for being "too negative".

Parts of *Safe As Milk*, Beefheart's first album, may have been recorded originally for A&M, but the version actually released by Buddah (which is how the company originally spelled its name) in late 1967 was the product of sessions at RCA's Hollywood studios that April. Beefheart was by then already straying a long way from the examples of early heroes Howlin' Wolf and John Lee Hooker, but a crucial factor held his wilder impulses in check.

That was the presence of the extraordinary young guitarist Ry Cooder, then just 20 years old, who effectively led the band, and even brought in session musicians as necessary. Cooder had made his name, along with Taj Mahal, in the group Rising Sons, and declined to appear in photos of the Magic Band. His guitar, however, permeates *Safe As Milk*. It's not always him playing lead, and he shifts to bass on a couple of tracks, but wherever you hear slide guitar – most notably, on the Delta-style, tone-setting opener Sure 'Nuff 'N Yes I Do – it's Cooder.

Even so, the lion's share of the credit for *Safe As Milk* belongs to Beefheart himself. He's often characterized as a non-musician and, apart from a one-off burst of blues harp and a couple of bass marimba contributions, he doesn't play an instrument on the album. His voice, however, is one of the great instruments of our time. His colossal vocal range has been estimated at up to seven octaves, but it's not exactly sweet and pure: one of the very few singers even to dare to model themselves on Howlin' Wolf, he's said to be able to break studio microphones at will. You can call his lyrics avant-garde poetry or psychedelic gibberish; what matters is the screaming, roaring, incantatory power of that voice.

Apart from one cover, Louisiana bluesman Robert Pete Williams' Grown So Ugly, Beefheart wrote or co-wrote every song. Cooder and producers Richard Perry and Bob Krasnow no doubt tightened the structures and arrangements, but the vision is Beefheart's. On Electricity, the real tour de force, he howls and chants above Cooder's haunting slide, backed by the unearthly wailing of a theremin, the Russian-invented electronic instrument from which sounds are coaxed by appropriately shamanistic hand-swirling. Other highlights include the pounding bass-drum rhythms of Abba Zaba and Zig Zag Wanderer, the mutated Jimmy Reed boogie of Plastic Factory, and the mock-pastoral weirdness of Autumn's Child. The CD ends with six "bonus" tracks from the later *Mirror Man* album, but with Cooder gone Beefheart was by then on the road to *Trout Mask Replica*.

➲ We almost chose **Rising Sons**, Sony, 1992

Leroy Carr

Sloppy Drunk

Catfish, 1999; recorded 1928–35

Quite why the pianist, singer and composer Leroy Carr doesn't have the profile he deserves is hard to say; he's a tragic lost genius to match any the blues has produced. Catfish's two-CD budget compilation **Sloppy Drunk** will surely help to redress the balance. Its 44 tracks represent roughly a quarter of Carr's output during a seven-year recording career that ended with his death from alcoholism at the age of 30. Their extraordinary range reveals Carr not only as a pioneer of citified blues – if his music was not exactly urban, it was certainly urbane – but also as a major influence on the rural Delta blues.

Carr himself did not come from the country, or even from the Deep South. Born in Nashville in 1905, he divided his youth between spells in the army, in prison, and travelling with a circus (one of his songs, not included here, is entitled "Carried Water For The Elephant"). In the late 1920s, he gravitated to Indianapolis, where he teamed up with guitarist Francis "Scrapper" Blackwell, a slightly older part-Cherokee guitarist from North Carolina. Brought together by their mutual interest in hard liquor – Blackwell as a bootlegger, Carr as an avid consumer – they became the greatest double act in the blues. Their musical styles were perfectly complementary, with Carr taking responsibility for the bass parts on the piano and providing lugubrious, bittersweet vocals, while Blackwell added expressive single-string runs on guitar. Blackwell was probably more talented as an instrumentalist, but Carr's solid sense of rhythm and pace, and skill as a songwriter, made him the dominant partner.

Blackwell being reluctant to neglect his moonshine business, the duo were first recorded by a Vocalion Records mobile unit in Indianapolis, in 1928. How Long – How Long Blues sold a million copies almost immediately, making it the first blues song to become a national hit. Down in Mississippi, its haunting refrain of "how long has that evening train been gone" struck a chord with both Muddy Waters and Robert Johnson.

Carr and Blackwell eagerly travelled to Vocalion's Chicago studios to capitalize on their success. Besides repeatedly recycling "How Long – How Long" – two more versions are included here – they reworked the train theme on songs like Tennessee Blues and Box Car Blues, as well as creating fascinating original compositions like the two-part Straight Alky Blues, with a lovely solo from Scrapper, and the charming stop-go Naptown Blues, which features a burst of scat singing from Leroy.

Carr's world-weary vocal style also lent itself to the "hokum" material characteristic of rivals Tampa Red and Georgia Tom, as on Gettin' All Wet. Elsewhere, he lets rip on proto-boogie numbers such as Baby Don't You Love Me No More and the Sloppy Drunk Blues itself ("I'd rather be sloppy drunk, than anything I know"). For Robert Johnson fans, Blues Before Sunrise, in which Carr laments having "such a miserable feeling, a feeling I do despise", may come as a real eye-opener. Johnson clearly set out to reproduce this entire sound – not just the piano and guitar lines, but the selfsame vocal inflections – on songs like "Kind Hearted Woman". Similarly, Prison Bound Blues, which opens "early one morning, the blues came falling down", is echoed in Johnson's "Me And The Devil".

Sloppy Drunk closes with all eight tracks from Carr and Blackwell's final session, in February 1935. Blackwell stormed out in the middle, leaving Carr to plough his way uncertainly through four solo pieces. The last, Six Cold Feet In The Ground, implored "just remember me, baby, when I'm in six feet of cold, cold ground." Two months later he was dead.

➲ We almost chose **Virtuoso Guitar Of Scrapper Blackwell**, Yazoo, 1991

Bo Carter

Banana In Your Fruit Basket

Yazoo, 1991; recorded 1931–36

Despite his undoubted status as one of the most talented, original and popular musicians on the pre-war blues scene, Bo Carter is seldom taken as seriously as he deserves. His "sin" was not merely that he saw himself as an entertainer, working for reward, but that he specialized in ribald sexual material. Most blues singers, of course, have always included sexual songs in their repertoires, but Carter built his career on them. As H.C. Speir, the Jackson store owner who first discovered him, put it, he was "the dirtiest man on record." Seventy years on, that's hardly much of a reason to condemn him without a hearing. In fact, on **Banana In Your Fruit Basket**, the music sounds as fresh as ever, and Carter's tuneful guitar-picking has a timeless appeal.

"Bo Carter" was the recording pseudonym of Armenter Chatmon. Born in 1893, he was one of the eleven sons of the well-known Mississippi musical family who provided the core of the Mississippi Sheiks and several other groups. Renowned live performers, the Chatmons played almost exclusively at "sociables" held for the white communities of local plantations, where country tunes and dance reels were more in demand than the blues. Armenter's guitar technique thus owed much more to fluent country finger-picking than to the slide or bottleneck styles of the Delta. Though he was also proficient on the violin, clarinet and banjo, he restricted himself as Bo Carter to the guitar alone, and recorded over a hundred sides from 1928 onwards.

Not all were risqué, by any means: he was the first person to record the beautiful "Corrina, Corrina", and may even have written it.

In his exemplary sleeve notes to *Banana In Your Fruit Basket*, Steve Calt sets out to place Carter's work in context, picking his way carefully through the minefield of racial and sexual attitudes both then and now. He argues that it's a mistake to think of sexual blues songs as being filled with double meanings when they were as a rule direct and unambiguous, and that what sound to modern ears like double entendres were often either the popular slang of the time or the results of censorship by white producers. He also points out that Carter's songs were intended for, and addressed to, female audiences as much as male.

With the exception of the exuberant **All Around Man**, in which Carter boasts that he can turn his hand to any profession you care to name – "I ain't no plumber, no plumber's son, I can do your screwing 'til the plumber-man comes" – he tends to stand slightly aloof from his material. Part of the pleasure comes from the contrast established between the actual words he's singing and the subdued delicacy of his guitar and his deadpan vocal delivery. Whether on **Don't Mash My Digger So Deep** ("if you don't want me to have your potatoes, don't mash my digger so deep") or **Pin In Your Cushion** ("let me stick my pin in your cushion, baby"), he portrays a perplexed innocence worthy of a great comedian. There's none of the misogyny or barely suppressed aggression that characterizes so much Delta blues; instead, we get the bemused regret of **My Pencil Won't Write No More** ("because the lead's all gone"), or the invocation of sex as a kind of magical balm, as in **Banana In Your Fruit Basket** itself: "let me put my banana in your fruit basket, then I'll be satisfied."

Though Bo Carter continued to record successfully until 1940, his star eventually waned. He spent his declining years as a blind street singer in Memphis, living in poverty just off Beale Street, and died in 1964.

⮱ We almost chose **Bo Carter's Advice**, Catfish, 2000

Albert Collins

Ice Pickin'

Alligator, 1987; recorded 1978

There's something strange about the way that Texan bluesman Albert Collins remains indelibly associated with freezing temperatures. As you might expect from Jimi Hendrix's favourite guitarist, there's every bit as much fire as ice about his playing. Yes, there's a cool, percussive precision to his soloing, hammered out with rock-hard fingers, but Collins was also a wild live performer, legendary for his crowd-pleasing "guitar walks" through audiences the world over.

Having started out in mid-1950s Houston playing keyboards, Collins switched to guitar aged 21, after his organ was stolen. Both his "cool sound" and his flamboyant style were originally modelled on stalwarts of the East Texan scene like T-Bone Walker and Clarence "Gatemouth" Brown, given a personal twist by his predilection for tuning to an open D-minor chord. Early singles like 1958's "The Freeze", on Kangaroo Records, and "Frosty", recorded for Beaumont's Hall-Way Records in 1962, earned him a reputation as "master of the Texas shuffle." Both were instrumentals, in part because of Collins' lack of faith in his own singing.

Collins remained very much a Texan artist until 1968, when Canned Heat took him under their wing and he was enthusiastically welcomed by the white audiences of California. Yet neither the three albums he recorded through the Canned Heat connection, nor his further studio work with Joe Walsh of the Eagles, brought him commercial success. That finally came when he teamed up with Alligator Records in the late 1970s after a period of disillusioned semi-retirement. The breakthrough record, **Ice Pickin'**, triggered a spate of equally accomplished releases that only ended with his premature death from liver cancer in 1993; it remains the definitive Albert Collins album, a career peak that highlights all his strongest qualities.

Collins said his sound "came from hanging around the horn sections of big bands", and *Ice Pickin'* is strongly reminiscent of Albert King's similarly horn-rich Stax recordings, with veteran Chicago saxophonist A.C. Reed providing a perfect foil for Collins' fretwork flurries. It's a joy to hear them trading phrases on **Ice Pick**, before Collins launches off into his solo. That's also the point where Collins' differences from King become clear; there's a manic and aggressive intensity that the laid-back King never matched.

Although Collins' guitar remains at centre stage throughout *Ice Pickin'*, variations of mood and pace keep matters consistently interesting. Thus the mournful **When The Welfare Turns Its Back On You** opens with the piercing, endless sustain of a single note, whereas during the blistering boogie of the closing instrumental, **Avalanche**, he must play the same note at least seventy times in quick-fire succession. At times, his singing tends to lack character, but those tracks where he resorts to his speaking voice instead – like the nine-minute **Conversation With Collins**, during which his guitar helps to play out the dialogue with his wife – work well. Even on throwaway numbers like **Too Tired** and **Master Charge**, enough personality still shines through to make the songs much more than just vehicles for his technical prowess.

For a man whose subsequent albums included *Frostbite, Frozen Alive!, Cold Snap* and *Iceman*, Collins showed comparative restraint by only including three tracks here that play on his usual cold motif. In all other respects, however, he let rip, fuelling a renaissance that was to see him win a Grammy for the *Showdown* album (with protégés Robert Cray and Johnny Copeland), play Live Aid with George Thorogood, and be an honoured guest of both John Lee Hooker (*Mr Lucky* and *Boom Boom*) and B.B. King (*Blues Summit*).

⊃ We almost chose **Deluxe Edition**, Alligator, 1997

Johnny Copeland

Honky Tonkin'

Bullseye Blues Classics, 1999; recorded 1981–89

Although Johnny Copeland counted as one of the brightest stars in the galaxy of Texan blues guitarists, his style was never quite distinctive enough to win him widespread recognition. Perhaps, in the final analysis, he lacked the sheer manic invention of his mentor T-Bone Walker, his friend and contemporary Albert Collins, or his disciple Stevie Ray Vaughan. To compensate for that, however, he offered an impassioned singing voice, superb songwriting skills and a burning desire to test the limits of the blues. During the 1980s, Copeland's liaison with Rounder Records finally gave him the creative scope he needed. **Honky Tonkin'**, a compilation that draws on five of his Rounder albums, provides a welcome opportunity to enjoy the results.

Copeland grew up in Louisiana, just east of the Texas state line, but he gravitated to Houston in 1950 at the age of 13. In his words, T-Bone Walker "was the man who made me interested in the blues." The young guitarist was soon touring statewide, backing Big Mama Thornton among others, and eventually landed a sixteen-year gig as the bandleader at Shady's Playhouse in Houston. Sadly, a steady stream of singles on local labels – including the magnificent "Every Dog's Got His Day" in 1969 – never translated into national success.

Houston's dwindling demand for the blues persuaded Copeland to relocate to New York in 1975, where hard work on the East Coast club circuit brought him to the attention of

Rounder Records. Johnny's first Rounder release, *Copeland Special*, saw him framed in a luxurious horn-rich setting reminiscent of the 1950s heyday of Texas's Duke and Peacock labels. **Down On Bended Knee**, a remake of one of his earlier Texan discs, features no fewer than four saxes, two trumpets and two trombones; he roars his heart out above the lot, like a grittier Bobby Bland, and wields a mean guitar into the bargain. **Everybody Wants A Piece Of Me** and **I Wish I Was Single** are equally powerful.

The follow-up, *Make My Home Where I Wear My Hat*, stuck to the same formula, with a sumptuous horn sound throughout. There's a particularly fine solo from Copeland on the title track, while **Devil's Hand** and **Honky Tonkin'** bristle with energy. But some of the subsequent Rounder albums failed to live up to that promise. On **Don't Stop By The Creek, Son** – one of two tracks here from 1983's *Texas Twister* – guest Stevie Ray Vaughan is soulless even by his standards. *Boom Boom*, in 1989, saw Copeland struggling to inspire his small, horn-free band to rise above routine run-throughs of their live standards.

Which makes it a shame that *Honky Tonkin'* only includes one cut from the intriguing 1985 album, *Bringin' It All Back Home*. Having become fascinated with African music during a ten-country tour of the continent in 1982, Copeland wrote several African-influenced pieces. His return visit to Sierra Leone two years later marked the first time an American blues artist had recorded in Africa. The infectious **Kasavubu**, on which Copeland's band was joined by half a dozen local musicians, was a triumph, with Johnny's exultant vocals weaving through a heady mix of horns, guitar and nonstop percussion.

Copeland revisited the African sound in 1996 on *Jungle Swing*, the better of his two 1990s albums for Verve. By then, however, he was seriously ill with a heart ailment. Although he managed to carry on touring even after he underwent a heart transplant at the start of 1997, he died on the operating table later that year.

➲ We almost chose **Bringin' It All Back Home**, Rounder, 1985

Robert Cray

Strong Persuader

Polygram, 1986

Listening to Robert Cray these days, it's hard to remember why certain die-hard purists greeted his arrival on the blues scene with such suspicion. There was a feeling perhaps that he hadn't paid the requisite dues, or that he played the blues as a canny career move rather than as his inescapable destiny. Now approaching 50 – though you'd never know it to look at that perennially youthful face – he's come a long way since those early days.

Certainly he wasn't your typical bluesman. Though born in Columbus, Georgia, he spent his childhood on assorted military bases in the US and Germany, before ending up as a teenager in Washington state. That makes him almost unique among major blues figures in not having grown up in the South. He was raised, moreover, on the Beatles rather than the blues. It's one of Cray's great strengths, however, that he's never pretended to be anything other than who he is. While rooting himself in the blues tradition, he's produced a deeply personal body of work that now stretches across a dozen consistently fine albums. Above all, he has addressed the concerns of his contemporaries rather than merely echoing the attitudes of the past. Just how much of a chord he can strike with his own peer group is demonstrated by the phenomenal success of his most perfectly realized album, **Strong Persuader**, which has remained in the blues best-seller lists ever since its release in 1986.

Neatly enough, Robert Cray received the decisive push that

directed his life towards the blues when Albert Collins played at his high-school graduation. Together with his boyhood friend Richard Cousins on bass, he was soon backing Collins on stage. He started recording under his own name for Atlantic in 1980, with *Who's Been Talking*, but the real breakthrough came – thanks to Collins once again – when Cray more than held his own alongside both Collins and Johnny Copeland on 1985's Grammy-winning three-way *Showdown!*

From the word go, Cray confessed that he was "caught between being a Blues man and a Soul man." His achievement on *Strong Persuader* was to draw on both those strands in creative tension, rather than get caught up with pointless pigeonholing. The musical formula of juxtaposing a lush, fluent lead guitar, backed by a solid blues-based rhythm section, against sassy soul-style horns, was not wildly original; in fact Cray used the Memphis Horns themselves, who'd established the template through so many '60s and '70s Stax sessions. Cray's warm, soulful singing perfectly complemented the mix, but even his voice was not exceptional.

What was new was the care that went into crafting and arranging the songs themselves, and above all the degree of introspection and emotional honesty in the actual words. Eschewing the swaggering and posturing of Chicago or the Delta, Cray opted instead for Californian self-analysis. He did so with considerable subtlety, too, as in the gentle irony of I Guess I Showed Her, or the way in which the "strong persuader" finds himself racked with guilt in Right Next Door (Because Of Me). It's all beautifully written, as for example in the powerful narrative of Foul Play.

That the ten tracks on *Strong Persuader* fit into just under forty minutes testifies to how well thought out the whole thing was. Everything's there for a purpose, and there's no room for empty histrionics. That still leaves scope for some flamboyant Cray guitar solos, however, as on Nothin' But A Woman, and the opening track Smoking Gun, which as a pop hit really made his name.

⮑ We almost chose **Take Your Shoes Off**, Ryko, 1999

Reverend Gary Davis

Pure Religion & Bad Company

Smithsonian/Folkways,1991; recorded 1957

To compare the music of blind guitarist Reverend Gary Davis – rooted in ragtime and dog-eared hymnals – with that of tortured Delta bluesmen such as Robert Johnson is like comparing chalk and cheese. Davis was, however, unquestionably one of the most gifted instrumentalists ever to work within the blues, capable of conjuring ethereal beauty with his nimble fingers. Though he preferred to regard himself as a gospel-playing evangelist, he's credited with spearheading the emergence of the "Piedmont blues" form in the Carolinas during the 1930s. That style in turn had such a major influence on the folk revival of the 1960s that it can be hard now to appreciate just how original and innovative Davis' playing was. **Pure Religion & Bad Company**, the third album of his career, recorded in New York in 1957, makes a wonderful place to start.

Born in South Carolina in 1896, Davis lost his sight before he reached adulthood, and became a street musician at an early age. The agility of his picking may be due to his having started out on banjo; his guitar style was not as percussive as that might imply, but he always had a meticulous sense of time, which allowed endless playful variations with rhythm. By the mid-1930s, he had teamed up in Durham, North Carolina, with Blind Boy Fuller and Sonny Terry. The three blind musicians lived in constant fear of losing their welfare payments if caught playing for tips. One of Davis' associates later recalled how much he outclassed his rivals by saying, "while you were playing one chord, Gary would play five"; another hailed him as "the playingest man I ever saw."

Fuller and Davis recorded together for ARC in New York in 1935, but Davis decided in mid-session that he would only perform spiritual material from then on. At around the same time he was ordained as a minister, but he continued to sing on the streets, now in the hope of saving souls. In fact, Davis didn't so much stop playing the blues as simply stop singing them. When he was encouraged to resume his recording career in the 1950s, his repertoire remained filled with blues material, which he'd perform as instrumentals.

That said, there's plenty of preaching on *Pure Religion and Bad Company*. Even before the guitar comes in on the opening track, **Pure Religion**, Davis declaims, "you must have religion in your soul", while the other title song, **Bad Company**, is a cautionary moral tale about a boy gone bad. The most compelling moments, however, come with the beautiful instrumental pieces such as **Hesitation Blues** and the irresistible dance tune **Buck Dance**. The picking on **Mountain Jack**, with its intricate runs and changes of tempo, is a special delight, while **Runnin' To The Judgement** nods a respectful head to the ragtime guitar of Blind Blake.

It would be unfair to say that the instrumentals are such a joy because of the deficiencies in Davis' singing voice – it may be gruff, but it's not in the Blind Willie Johnson league. Davis was also a master at interweaving between his vocal and his guitar lines. Yet the mood is definitely different on the sung tracks, as with the pained, searingly slow **Moon Goes Down**. **Candy Man** is played differently from the more familiar Mississippi John Hurt versions, but it's still bawdier than you'd expect of a reverend, with its "run and get the pitcher, get the baby some beer" refrain.

Davis continued to play, record and teach until his death in 1972, and all his albums are worth having. For breathtaking guitar work, however, there's no beating *Pure Religion & Bad Company*.

➲ We almost chose **O Glory, The Apostolic Studio Sessions**, Genes, 1996

Guitar Slim

The Things That I Used To Do

Ace, 1987; recorded 1953–55

The fact that Jimi Hendrix started out playing guitar with Little Richard's band in the early 1960s is mind-boggling enough. Now cast your mind back ten years earlier still, and picture the two performers rolled into one – the screeching distorted guitar sound, the shrieking gospel-imbued vocals, the wild clothes, the flamboyant stage presence . . . the lot. That's Guitar Slim.

The brightest, gaudiest star to burst across the blues firmament during the 1950s, Slim has sadly missed out on the acclaim he deserves. Perhaps he peaked a little too early to get swept along by the rock'n'roll boom, or maybe he was too off the wall to fit in anywhere; in any case, he drank himself to death before the decade was out. His monument endures, however, in a clutch of classic titles cut for Specialty Records, now collected on the Ace anthology **The Things That I Used To Do**.

Guitar Slim was born plain Eddie Jones in Greenwood, Mississippi, in 1926, and raised by his grandfather on a nearby plantation after his mother died when he was 5. A childhood familiarity with church music is self-evident from his recordings, but the young Slim is better remembered as the coolest dancer for miles around. He started his career dancing with a travelling blues troupe, then graduated first to singing and finally playing the guitar; when he hit the New Orleans scene in 1950, he was doing all three at once. Slim outdid his hero, Texas bluesman T-Bone Walker, by dyeing his hair green or blue and wearing mismatching suits in equally lurid colours. His showstopper on club dates was to charge through his audience and out onto the street, still playing with his guitar plugged into a 350-foot lead.

A 1950 newspaper review described Slim, then working with a trio that included Huey "Piano" Smith, as an "exact copy of Gatemouth Brown." His first recordings, for Imperial in 1951 and Bullet in Nashville in 1952, created little stir, but in late 1953 he had the great fortune to be teamed up by Specialty with a young blind pianist who had fallen on hard times in New Orleans – Ray Charles. The session that produced The Things That I Used To Do itself is the stuff of legend. This was Charles' first gig as an arranger, and he framed Slim's impassioned slow vocal amid sumptuous, stately horns, then allowed his guitar to run free. It took several dozen takes to get things just right; you can hear the relief in Charles' cry of "yeah" in the last bar. Art Rupe, the boss of Specialty, called it "the worst piece of shit" he'd ever heard, but it sold a million at the time, and is now hailed as one of the seminal moments in which the blues and gospel begat soul.

Slim cut three more self-penned masterpieces during that same session: Letter To My Girlfriend, Well I Done Got Over It, and the extraordinary The Story Of My Life, which in addition to its searing lyrics has a piercing guitar solo that sounds uncannily like Jimi Hendrix. Without producer Johnny Vincent, let alone Ray Charles, he couldn't quite match that achievement on his next studio date, but he did come up with another powerful slow blues number, Sufferin' Mind. His subsequent Specialty releases varied between attempts to recapture the magic of "Things", as with Something To Remember You By; gritty autobiographical material like Guitar Slim; and the kind of gospel-styled workouts that Little Richard was soon to start recording for the same label, including Think It Over and Quicksand. As his sales declined, Slim was lured away to join Atco, a subsidiary of Atlantic, in 1956, but he never recaptured his early success and died in 1959.

⊃ We almost chose **Sufferin' Mind**, Specialty, 1991

Buddy Guy

The Complete Chess Studio Recordings

Chess, 1992; recorded 1960–67

Buddy Guy is the last of the great Chess bluesmen and the only one still recording into the twenty-first century; his seven-year stint with Chess, however, was far from commercially successful. Considering his abundant talents as both guitarist and singer, he was woefully under-recorded. The one consolation is that at least his entire Chess output fits onto a two-CD collection, **The Complete Chess Studio Recordings.** With a total of 47 tracks, ten of them previously unreleased and several more all but unobtainable, it combines a dozen or so tight, focused blues classics with all manner of fascinating experiments, outtakes and downright fripperies.

George "Buddy" Guy was born in 1936 to a sharecropping family in rural Louisiana. He acquired his first acoustic guitar at 13 – on a trip to Memphis – just in time to learn John Lee Hooker's sensational new "Boogie Chillen". Having cut his teeth in Baton Rouge (playing alongside the likes of Slim Harpo), Guy moved north to Chicago just as soon as he was old enough to get into the city's clubs. The precocious 21-year-old swiftly hooked up with Otis Rush and Magic Sam as the three lions who established the so-called "West Side sound". Times were hard, however, until the oft-recounted day when Muddy Waters presented the starving Guy with a salami sandwich and conferred on him the status of honorary "son".

Guy joined the Chess "family" in 1960, after his previous label, Cobra, became abruptly defunct when its owner was found floating in Lake Michigan. His principal role was as a side-man; the *Complete Recordings* are those he made under his own name, not his contributions to such sessions as Muddy Waters' *Folk Singer* album and Koko Taylor's "Wang Dang Doodle". According to Willie Dixon, Guy lacked impact as a solo artist because he sounded too much like B.B. King; Guy himself insists that it was because Leonard Chess wouldn't let him play the way he wanted. Above all, Guy loved to play *loud*; he was only vindicated when artists like Hendrix and Clapton were hailed as superstars for playing in Guy's style. Chess eventually admitted his mistake: "that shit you've been trying to sell me is selling like hot shit and I've been fucking dumb."

If any of that implies that Guy's Chess work was some sort of disappointment, then just listen to the opening track, **First Time I Met The Blues**. A deeply traditional blues written by Little Brother Montgomery, who also provides piano flourishes, Guy's luscious guitar and gospel-tinged vocals simply soar above three stately saxes and Fred Below's tub-thumping drums. Other unquestionable masterpieces include **My Time After Awhile**, from a session watched by the young Rolling Stones in 1964; the tortured **Hard But It's Fair**; and the seven-minute epic **Stone Crazy**, which, thanks to its sustained soloing (virtually unprecedented in 1961), was the only one that sold in any quantity.

What's most exciting about this collection, though, is that you never know what's coming up next. There's pure throwaway pop, like the novelty dance number **Slop Around**, the messy **Gully Hully**, and the shoo-wopping **Lip Lap Louie**. There's finger-snapping jazz, in the shape of the Art Blakey standard **Moanin'**, with its cool sax, piano and bass riffing, and off-the-wall go-go jingles like **American Bandstand** and **Untitled Instrumental**. Only when Guy finally left Chess in 1967 did he also give up his day job, working in a garage. On his swansong, the infernally funky **Buddy's Groove**, he sounds exactly like Jimi Hendrix. It was time to get out on the road.

➲ We almost chose **Buddy's Blues**, Chess, 1997

Buddy Guy

Buddy's Baddest

Silvertone, 1999; recorded 1991–99

It's easy to think of "paying their dues" as something bluesmen had to do in the bad old days. Buddy Guy was doing it right up until the 1990s. After his youthful taste of a little fame and even less fortune at Chess (see p.35), it took a long, hard 25-year slog to win him the recognition he deserved. Along the way, he made several fine albums, both alone and in partnership with his Chicago cohort Junior Wells, but by the time of *Damn Right, I've Got The Blues*, his 1991 debut for Silvertone Records, he hadn't had a US album release for ten years. Since then, there's been no looking back.

Silvertone's "rediscovery" of Buddy Guy came in the wake of John Lee Hooker's 1989 success with *The Healer*, and followed a similar trajectory. *Damn Right* abounded in celebrity cameos from the likes of Eric Clapton, Jeff Beck and Mark Knopfler, and scooped up a Grammy. More big-name guests, such as Paul Rodgers and Travis Tritt, jumped on the bandwagon for 1993's follow-up *Feels Like Rain*. which earned Guy another Grammy, and there were three further new Silvertone releases during the 1990s.

Buddy's Baddest collects tracks from all five albums, plus three first-rate previously unreleased numbers, to create a 76-minute extravaganza of top-volume, full-throated contemporary blues from one of the music's true originals. It's not all good – combine Guy's penchant for noisy histrionics with his determination to please a crossover rock audience, and sometimes the results have all the finesse of a sledgehammer – but at its best his guitar work is a sheer joy. He can justly claim to have invented the kind of string-bending, single-note, ultra-fluid soloing that pours out of almost every track, and he's still doing it a whole lot better than his Johnny-come-lately competitors.

Inevitably, the most powerful moment comes with the song that started it all, **Damn Right, I've Got The Blues**. Guy's opening guitar notes are a piercing clarion call, while the thunderous aggrieved roar of his singing is utterly compelling. Whatever the lyrics may claim to be about, it's an irresistible demand for respect.

Buddy's Baddest abounds in inspired retreads of blues standards. His own **My Time After Awhile**, drawn from the *Real Deal* live album, gets a sumptuous eight-minute treatment, his restrained, expressive solos embellished by Johnnie Johnson on piano while the horn-rich Saturday Night Live Band provides multitextured support. Guy's much-noted resemblance to B.B. King is undeniable at such points, which makes it a particular delight on **She's Nineteen Years Old** to hear his adult voice sound so exactly like his mentor Muddy Waters. There's more Muddy in the closing medley, **Innocent Man**, which incorporates segments of Waters' "Mannish Boy" along with Wolf's "Backdoor Man", while other successful covers include **Five Long Years**, **Mustang Sally**, Roosevelt Sykes' **Miss Ida B** and Little Willie John's **I Need Your Love So Bad**.

Now and then, Guy's urge to out-gun Jimi Hendrix and Stevie Ray Vaughan gets the better of him. Denise LaSalle's **Someone Else Is Steppin' In** gains nothing from being bludgeoned half to death, but most of the more indulgent excesses of the Silvertone albums have been omitted. The only duet included, **Feels Like Rain**, with Bonnie Raitt, is low on subtlety but it's still an atmospheric, classy slice of pop blues. On **Midnight Train**, from *Heavy Love*, Buddy tussles amiably with wunderkind Jonny Lang, making it clear who's boss while still keeping things fun and funky. In the end, so what if he misfires from time to time? We can only be thankful that he's still got way too much life in him to go down the dignified elder statesman route just yet.

⟳ We almost chose **Damn Right, I've Got The Blues**, Silvertone, 1991

Slim Harpo

The Best Of Slim Harpo

Hip-O, 1997; recorded 1957–67

Considering it's sandwiched between Mississippi and Texas, Louisiana's contributions to the blues has been relatively insubstantial; the musicians of New Orleans have been too busy doing their own thing. The genre of "swamp blues", however, in which the angst and urgency of Chicago blues are replaced by a laid-back but naggingly infectious drone, could only have arisen in Louisiana. Its greatest exponent, Slim Harpo, combined a mastery of the heavily amplified harmonica-driven boogie rhythms of men like Jimmy Reed and Little Walter with a blessed knack for writing simple, catchy hit songs. On top of that, his collected works make eerie listening as a virtual blue-print for the sound and attitude of his close contemporaries, the Rolling Stones.

James Moore, who was born in 1924 in Lobdell, Louisiana, right across the Mississippi River from Baton Rouge, played his earliest gigs as Harmonica Slim. When he came to make his first solo recordings, for the Crowley-based Excello label in 1957, the existence of an already-established namesake on the West Coast forced him to swap things around a little, and he became Slim Harpo.

Few recording careers can have opened more confidently than Harpo's. Even before the music starts on his very first song, he declaims "Well I'm a king bee"; and then the steady bass beat kicks in, beefed up by pounding, muffled drum slaps in the background. The Rolling Stones appropriated **I'm A King Bee** almost note for note on their own first LP in 1964. Mick Jagger even interjected the same "buzz a while" admonition to the band, although in the process he managed to transmute Harpo's slow, insouciant Southern drawl into a sort of fey mid-Atlantic Cockney yelping. No one put it better than Jagger himself: "what's the point of listening to us doing 'I'm A King Bee' when you can listen to Slim Harpo doing it?".

Not that Harpo's nasal singing style was entirely natural. Producer Jay Miller reportedly found his "ordinary" voice so unappealing that he suggested he sing through his nose instead. The resultant resemblance to Hank Williams was no coincidence and does much to explain the ready crossover appeal of Harpo's music.

While "I'm A King Bee" was a regional hit, Harpo's first taste of national success came with **Rainin' In My Heart** in 1961. A slower ballad, characterized by a looping Fats-Domino-like rhythm, this smothered a similar, lazy vocal line with some deliciously mournful blues harp. Royalty disputes restricted his visits to the studio over the next few years, and a number of formulaic follow-ups failed to chart. Of his various reworkings of the bee theme, only the lively 1963 instrumental **Buzzin'** is included in this collection. His biggest-selling record of all, **Baby Scratch My Back**, came along in 1965. Described by Harpo himself as "an attempt at rock'n'roll", it was heralded as a slice of proto-funk, and Harpo gained major exposure in appearances with the James Brown Revue.

In 1966, he went back to the boogie with **Shake Your Hips**, and was dismissed as dated for his troubles. It now sounds like his masterpiece, a funky, soupy and insistent development of his original style that once more served as a prototype for the Rolling Stones, who produced a lovingly murky cover on their seminal 1972 album, *Exile on Main Street*. By then, tragically, Harpo was dead, having suffered a heart attack at the age of 46 in early 1970, just as he was about to embark on his first European tour.

⮑ We almost chose **Sting It Then**, Ace, 1998

21

Corey Harris

Greens From The Garden

Alligator, 1999

You can tell the blues are entering a new era when a young blues artist is pictured on a CD cover wearing dreadlocks in a topknot, and proclaims that he "grew up listening to rap." Corey Harris was born in 1969, raised in Denver not the Delta, and graduated in Anthropology in Maine. Add lengthy stints in Cameroon and the Cajun country of Louisiana, and you're clearly going to get a postmodern take on the blues.

On both his first two albums for Alligator Records, 1995's *Between Midnight And Day* and 1997's *Fish Ain't Bitin'*, Corey positioned himself as a standard-bearer for the classic blues tradition. The first consisted almost entirely of solo cover versions of songs by the likes of Charlie Patton and Bukka White, while the second won the W.C. Handy award for Acoustic Blues Album Of The Year. More than half of the tracks on *Fish* were self-penned, however, and it also featured contributions from the brass-band musicians Harris had met while playing on the streets of New Orleans.

While Harris had always reinterpreted his source material through the prism of his own experience, rather than merely copying old records, with **Greens From The Garden** he was determined to take things a stage further. The "greens" motif, as brought out by the sleeve photos of Harris standing in an endless fertile field, and the snatches of "found" dialogue and recipes interspersed between the tracks, suggests the abundance of potential ingredients that can go into the pot. Eschewing simple categorizations, the album shows him ranging across a variety of genres, and performing both acoustic and electric music, alone and in tandem with colleagues from other disciplines. It also highlights his developing skills as a songwriter, with new work in French as well as English, and Jamaican patois as well as the time-honoured voice of the Delta. By no stretch of the imagination is this a traditional blues album, but Harris remains rooted in the blues even as he's creating an exciting prototype for the music's new millennium.

Two luscious solo renditions of blues standards, delivered on Harris' National resophonic guitar, serve as reminders of his credentials: Tampa Red's (and B.B. King's) **Sweet Black Angel** and Blind Blake's **Diddy Wah Diddy**. Two group performances, by contrast, bring the blues bang up to date. **Basehead**, the opening track, warns of the peril of crack cocaine – "seen the devil last night, walk like a natural man, had a pipe in his mouth, a rock in his hand" – atop a frenzied Bo Diddley beat. **Lynch Blues** is a chilling reworking of the "strange fruit" theme, set to a John Lee Hooker boogie, on which Harris roars like a full-strength Muddy Waters. There's a less intense atmosphere to the beautifully finger-picked **Nola Rag**, an affectionate tribute to the young lions of New Orleans' brass-band scene, and the closing "bonus" track, **Teabag Blues**, in which Harris duets with Billy Bragg on his own arrangement of Woody Guthrie's lyrics.

All the cross-genre shifts are pulled off with appealing confidence. **Wild West**, another Harris morality tale, is backed by a powerful reggae rhythm, and the brass-band standard **Just A Closer Walk With Thee**, dedicated to King Selassie I, is given an even more satisfying Rastafarian twist. **Eh La Bas** is a good-time Cajun anthem, while **Pas Parlez** presumably belongs to that little-known subgenre, Cameroonian waltz. Two live tracks from the Funky Butt in New Orleans, **Congo Square Rag** and the raucous instrumental **Honeysuckle**, feature Harris alongside pianist Henry Butler, and point the way to their two-man follow-up, released in 2000, *vu-du-menz*.

➲ We almost chose **Fish Ain't Bitin'**, Alligator, 1997

22

Alvin Youngblood Hart

Territory

Hannibal, 1998

Alvin Youngblood Hart first dedicated himself to playing acoustic blues in the mid-1980s, before the word "unplugged" was a glint in a marketing man's eye. As a young black Californian aspiring to be a blues musician, he was an even rarer breed then than he is today. While his passion for the prewar country blues may border on the obsessive – it extends to restoring the instruments on which the music was played – it produces richly satisfying results. No dry-as-dust purist, his sheer love of sound entices him into exploring not only what the blues has been in the past, but its potential for the twenty-first century.

Though he's a native of Oakland, Hart's upbringing incorporated high school in Chicago, and extended family stays at his grandmother's home in the hill country of Mississippi. His initiation as a musician came from hanging out on Chicago's famous Maxwell Street, but disillusionment with the band scene soon led him to perform solo. It proved so hard to make a living that he signed up with the Coast Guard for a seven-year stint that saw him stationed on a riverboat at Natchez on the Mississippi River. Recognition only came with a move back to California, where he was spotted in 1995 supporting Taj Mahal and fell into the orbit of the Grateful Dead. A contract with the revitalized OKeh record label bore fruit in his well-received 1996 debut release *Big Mama's Door*. An entirely acoustic collection that included covers of songs by Leadbelly, Charlie Patton and Blind Willie McTell, it was nominated for numerous awards.

Territory, Hart's second album, came out on Hannibal in 1998 to a generally favourable reception. While *Living Blues* named it their Best Blues Album Of The Year, some critics charged Hart with having lost his direction. Certainly it's less wholeheartedly devoted to the blues than *Big Mama's Door*, and shows Hart widening his focus to taken in a broad range of American folk musics, including country and western swing. Not all of his experiments work, with lesser moments including an unimaginative slice of big-band ska, Just About To Go, and a Captain Beefheart cover, Ice Rose, that's neither acoustic nor even particularly listenable.

At its best, however, *Territory* is magical. The perfect place to start is the gorgeous rendition of Illinois Blues, which is at once a faithful reproduction of Skip James' original and a resetting of its eerie atmosphere into a modern context. Both Hart and his wife are expert guitar technicians, and he conjures a sumptuous slow, rolling sound from his resonator guitar. On Mama Don't Allow, a traditional dance piece recorded by Papa Charlie Jackson and Cow Cow Davenport in the 1920s – and "sampled" by John Lee Hooker in "Boogie Chillen" – that same richness of tone permeates the boogie rhythm, but this time it's embellished with slide effects on the upper strings. A third blues standard, the ballad John Hardy, is adorned by a tasteful solo on, of all things, the concertina.

While the gentle swing of Dancing With Tears In My Eyes is another highlight, Hart's self-penned songs more than hold their own. As well as two ballads, the affectionate Sallie, Queen Of The Pines and the ominous narrative Countrycide, on which his twelve-string dobro is backed by Josh Jones' congas, he contributes a couple of delightful country-flavoured instrumentals, Tallacatcha and Ouachita Run, featuring Brian Godchaux on fiddle. Even so, while Hart's 2000 follow-up, *Start With The Soul*, explores ever more eclectic directions, *Territory* remains the album of a man still enamoured of his first love – the blues.

➲ We almost chose **Big Mama's Door**, OKeh, 1996

23

Z.Z. Hill

Greatest Hits

Malaco, 1990; recorded 1980–84

With his unexpected 1980s success for Mississippi's Malaco Records, Z.Z. Hill almost single-handedly kept the flame of the blues alight through the biggest slump in its history. In certain quarters his success was regarded as merely lucky – as though the fact that other, arguably finer, blues singers languished in obscurity was somehow his fault. While his vocal style may not have been utterly original, he was an extraordinarily effective and engaging performer whose achievement, above all, was to prove that the blues remained relevant to black adult audiences. Prowling the hinterland between blues and soul, Hill chronicled and castigated the infidelities and insecurities of his contemporaries in a way that was as much concerned with joy as with pain.

A native of Texas, Arzell "Z.Z." Hill was in his mid-forties when he signed to Malaco in 1980. A veteran of major labels such as Atlantic, United Artists and Columbia, he had already made several classic recordings. In the absence of a career-spanning anthology that would take in such earlier singles as "This Time They Told The Truth" and "Love Is So Good When You're Stealing It", Malaco's **Greatest Hits** compilation is the best place to get a sense of Hill's achievement – despite the fact that it's only 43 minutes long and its eleven tracks provide only a brief overview.

The idea at Malaco was to move Hill away from his recent disco-influenced material and re-ground him in the blues. With

Down Home Blues, an unabashed celebration of his return to a familiar old blues style, the scheme paid off beyond anyone's wildest expectations. The song was the title track of his second album and it remained in Billboard's soul charts for over a hundred weeks. The protagonist on "Down Home Blues" is female and Hill's primary appeal was always to Southern black women. Even more intriguingly, on the smash hit **Someone Else Is Steppin' In**, Denise LaSalle's original was only minimally adapted and most of what Hill sings is quoted female speech. The effect is startling and it is hard not to double-take as Hill growls "I'm a brand new woman, as anyone can see."

Z.Z. Hill's great obsession was adultery. He may not overtly approve of it, but he sees it everywhere and his pleas for his woman not to stray rest on the bedrock of his own guilt. From the very first track, the funky **Cheatin' In The Next Room**, he wears his doubts on his sleeve: he knows his woman has been faking and is even now "making plans to go out and do wrong." **Three Into Two Won't Go** boasts the quintessential Hill line, "you're carrying a baby, is it his or mine?", and this theme of anxiety culminates in the magnificently paranoid **Open House At My House**, in which he's convinced that "the whole neighborhood" – from the clerk at the service station to the preacher – "has been dipping in my sugar bowl." The song had previously been recorded by Little Johnny Taylor, whose minings of the same mother lode remain a staple of the Southern airwaves to this day.

As a vocalist, gliding from a croon to a rasp, Hill owes most to the influence of Bobby Bland. On **Get A Little, Give A Little** – a direct manifesto for his female constituents, be they "nurse, secretary, waitress or clerk" – he even essays one or two of Bland's trademark throaty gargles. That Malaco's musicians provided the perfect backing, with the solid, driving rhythm section backed by horns and strings where appropriate, was evidenced by Bland's own move to the label in 1985, a year after Hill's cruelly early death.

➲ We almost chose **In Memorium**, Malaco, 1995

24

Earl Hooker

Simply The Best

MCA, 1999; recorded 1956–69

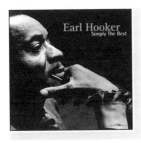

Almost all the figures who spring to mind as great blues guitarists tend to have been singers as well. But the man who made his guitar "speak" most eloquently of all lacked confidence in his own singing voice. Earl Hooker never became a major star, despite acclaim from B.B. King, Buddy Guy, and Junior Wells, who said of him: "Earl Hooker could do more with a guitar than a monkey could do with a coconut." This is partly due to his premature death but more because so much of his finest work was done as a sideman to other, bigger names.

Earl Zebedee Hooker, also known as "Zeb", a first cousin to John Lee Hooker, was born in Clarksdale, Mississippi, in 1930. Taught slide guitar by Robert Nighthawk, he was also heavily influenced by white country musicians like Merle Travis. By 1950, he was performing behind Sonny Boy Williamson II on the radio. He briefly recorded with both King in 1952 and Sun in 1953, before he relocated to Chicago and established his own band, the Roadmasters.

Simply The Best is a sumptuous 76-minute showcase of Hooker in all his glory, ranging from the pure Delta-derived slide guitar of his Chicago years to electrifying effects-laden post-psychedelic wig-outs. Contrary to first impressions, however, it scarcely covers his entire career. All except three of its nineteen tracks were recorded in California in 1969, and at least seven on the same day. They date from Hooker's final extraordinary efflorescence, when he cut no fewer than eight albums within a six-month period, less than a year before he died of tuberculosis.

Simply The Best starts by setting out Hooker's credentials in the most definitive conceivable way, with Muddy Waters' seminal **You Shook Me**. If you knew no better, you'd swear it was Muddy playing that piercing slide intro. In fact, Waters overdubbed his vocal in 1962 onto one of several 1961 Hooker instrumentals that had been bought up by Chess; his "You Need Love", which became Led Zeppelin's "Whole Lotta Love", was another.

Next up come a couple of early instrumentals released under Hooker's own name; **Frog Hop**, made for Argo in 1956, and **Tanya**, a Checker single from 1962 with a bizarre synthesized pedal-steel sound. All the rest of the album is drawn from Hooker's 1969 West Coast sessions, which included two solo albums and six with other artists. It makes amazing listening: while still rooted in the Delta, Hooker had become fascinated with new technology such as wah-wah pedals and fuzzboxes, and had clearly been listening to a lot of Jimi Hendrix. Whoever's name happened to be on the final product, it was all Hooker's show – he simply erupted all over everything.

On his Blue Thumb album *Sweet Black Angel*, Hooker was produced and backed by his early Clarksdale protégé, Ike Turner, as he unleashed his powers on standards like **Drivin' Wheel** and **Sweet Home Chicago**, a veritable feast of fuzz. *Don't Have To Worry*, for ABC/Bluesway, was even more extravagant, with jaw-dropping solos on numbers like **You Got To Lose** and **Universal Rock**.

For all Hooker's virtuosity, his collaborations here are notable above all for their sheer weirdness. Accompanying former bandmate Johnny "Big Moose" Walker on **The Sky Is Crying**, his at first impeccable slide gradually mutates into the honkings of a brontosaurus deep in some primeval swamp. Joining his cousin his **Messin' With The Blues** and **If You Miss 'Im, I Got 'Im**, Earl's demented wah-wah soars above John Lee's trademark soupy boogie, punctuated by growls of "don't mess with the Hookers."

➲ We almost chose **There's A Fungus Among Us**, Red Lightnin', 2000

25

John Lee Hooker

The Legendary Modern Recordings

Virgin, 1994; recorded 1948–54

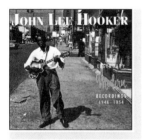

Rooted at the very heart of the blues and yet uniquely idiosyncratic, John Lee Hooker is the most charismatic and compelling blues artist of the last sixty years. Working in two main styles – churning out his mesmeric up-tempo "endless boogie" or stamping his way through brooding slow blues numbers – he has always been as much shaman as showman. Some call his music "deep funk"; Miles Davis said he was "the funkiest man alive." Others think of him as the most African of bluesmen and argue that his songs use an African-style pentatonic scale rather than the European seven-note diatonic scale. Hooker himself has little time for such niceties. Counting the bars or the beats comes a distant second to maintaining the passionate intensity of his message, and his finest songs have an incantatory power that transcends specific lyrics or tunes. As **The Legendary Modern Recordings** reveals, that power was there from the moment he first entered a recording studio back in 1948.

Though the exact year remains disputed, John Lee Hooker was born in the Mississippi Delta, just south of Clarksdale, around 1917. His father, William Hooker, was a preacher adamantly opposed to the blues, but when his parents separated during his early teens John chose to live with his mother. Her new partner, Will Moore, not only taught the boy to play guitar, but, as Charles Shaar Murray describes in his superb Hooker biography, "gave him the boogie." While Moore played alongside Delta bluesmen like Charlie Patton, his town of origin was Shreveport, and he imbued John with the rhythms of Louisiana as much as the traditions of Mississippi.

John Lee Hooker moved to Memphis at 16, then to Cincinnati before reaching Detroit in the early 1940s. He spent his days working as a janitor and his nights playing the clubs until a record-store audition introduced him to Bernie Besman of the local Sensation label. His first session resulted in the epic anthem **Boogie Chillen**. Over an insistent rhythm, Hooker tells of his initial encounter with the nightlife of Detroit's Hasting Street, and recalls overhearing his father telling his mother: "Let that boy boogie-woogie, because it's in him, and it's got to come out." A defining moment in popular music history, the song sold over a million copies: "it was a big, big, big hit. Boy, everywhere you went it was all you could hear."

Besman leased Hooker's debut discs to the larger Modern label to ensure national distribution while continuing to act as producer. Hooker now bitterly rejects Besman's claim to have shaped his style – and his entitlement to shared writing credits – but the two created a wonderful sound together. On live dates Hooker was already working with a band, but Besman recorded him solo, and filled out the tracks with cavernous echo. John Lee provided his own percussion by stamping on the floor, sometimes with bottle tops on his shoes, and in due course Besman learned to mike a sheet of plywood at his feet. **Crawling King Snake** is the most famous of these early classics, but several lesser-known tracks from 1949, including the instrumental **Hoogie Boogie** and the ominous **Drifting From Door To Door**, are stunning.

In 1951, joined by Eddie Kirkland as second guitarist, Hooker recorded his second million-seller. Inspired by Glenn Miller's "In The Mood" – or at least by its title – **I'm In The Mood** was given an extra depth by overdubbing three layers of vocals. When Besman and Hooker parted company soon afterwards, in part because of Hooker's persistent recording for other labels, John promptly signed to Modern itself. The final eight of the 24 tracks here stem from that period.

⮕ We almost chose **The Early Years**, Tomato, 1994

26

John Lee Hooker

The Very Best Of John Lee Hooker

Rhino, 1995; recorded 1948–87

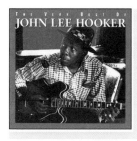

John Lee Hooker has been making records for well over fifty years, and at least fifty of his CDs are still on the market. Where to begin your Hooker collection is easy enough – with *The Legendary Modern Recordings*, as described on p.49 – but the vast central span of his career can be bewildering. Hooker himself didn't exactly have his eyes on history: during the 1950s, in particular, he recorded for anybody and everybody. His pseudonyms ranged from the transparent John Lee Booker to Texas Slim, Birmingham Sam, and even Little Pork Chops. "I didn't care what they called me . . . If they'd pay me, I'd play." Not only did his work appear on a plethora of labels but it might subsequently be relicensed to some other company and come out again years later. Atlantic, Stax and Chess all released Hooker albums bought in from elsewhere.

Rhino have done a great job of picking their way through this labyrinth to create anthologies of Hooker's finest hours, with the single-volume **The Very Best Of John Lee Hooker** making a near-perfect introduction. Its fifteen tracks kick off, naturally enough, with the cream of the Modern sessions: **Boogie Chillen**, **Crawling King Snake**, **Hobo Blues** and **I'm In The Mood**. Also from that era, but originally released on Sensation, is the fabulous **Huckle Up Baby**, a twanging, stomping free-form interpretation of Paul "Hucklebuck" Williams' 1948 hit "The Hucklebuck".

Another classic example of what biographer Charles Shaar Murray refers to as "Hookerization" – the process by which John

Lee would deconstruct and reassemble his own and other artists' songs – follows next. **I Need Some Money** is a beautiful 1960 reinvention of Berry Gordy's then-recent "Money (That's What I Want)", with Hooker taking the song at his own leisurely pace on acoustic guitar, while the rhythm section from jazzman Cannonball Adderley's band provide sympathetic backing.

"Money" was cut during a brief hiatus in Hooker's productive liaison with the Vee Jay label. His two most enduring monuments from that period were two very similar pop-influenced hits, which are as close as he ever came to recording conventional twelve-bar blues. **Dimples** dates from 1956, while **Boom Boom**, which edged its way into the pop charts, was made in 1962 with the Motown house band. Perhaps the most surprising moment on this CD is the exuberant **Shake It Baby**, recorded after hours in Hamburg, Germany, in 1962, during Hooker's first European tour. A massive European hit, it was clearly modelled on "What'd I Say", but while it's John Lee who's howling like Ray Charles, amazingly enough it's guitarist T-Bone Walker who's egging him on from the piano stool. Further highlights from the 1960s include two cuts from the Chess album, *The Real Folk Blues*, **You Know, I Know** and **One Bourbon, One Scotch, One Beer**, and a chilling live performance of **I'm Bad Like Jesse James**. The final treat comes from 1987, in the shape of Hooker singing Robert Johnson's **Terraplane Blues**, accompanied by Roy Rogers on slide guitar.

Most powerful of all, however, is the astonishing **Burning Hell**, from the *Hooker'N'Heat* album, which teamed Hooker with American blues-rockers Canned Heat in May 1970. Hooker is very much in the driving seat during this re-exploration of a theme he'd first recorded in 1949, propelling things forward with his insistent foot-stamping as much as his powerhouse guitar, but he's spurred ever higher by the urgent harmonica vamping of Alan Wilson. The song culminates with a triumphant rejection of the power of religion to intimidate, as Hooker cries, "ain't no hell." Ironically, by the time "Burning Hell" was released, Wilson had died in an apparent suicide.

⊃ We almost chose **The Ultimate Collection**, Rhino, 1991

27

John Lee Hooker

Mr Lucky

Silvertone, 1991; recorded 1990–91

There's something rather ironic about John Lee Hooker finally earning his just rewards as the great collaborator, fêted by rock stars and releasing a succession of best-selling albums studded with contributions from special guests. If asked in the mid-1980s to predict which blues artist might make such a comeback, Hooker's name would not have sprung to mind. While his recordings remained greatly respected, Hooker himself had always been seen as a self-evident one-off, and notoriously difficult to accompany. Yes, he'd worked alongside jazz, blues, soul and rock bands as well as performing solo, but his music had retained its integrity throughout. No rock musicians had been able to build their own careers by "lifting" Hooker's sound, any more than Hooker could step away from his own self and find a new audience. As Keith Richards put it, "you're not going to mistake John Lee Hooker for anyone else."

With his 1989 album *The Healer*, however, Hooker gained a new lease of life at the age of over 70. Produced by Californian blues guitarist Roy Rogers, and benefiting especially from Carlos Santana's input on the title track, it won him a Grammy and kick-started a lucrative career as the world's favourite veteran bluesman. Hooker had become an icon.

Just because his records started to sell again doesn't prove they were better than before, of course. Hooker as an old man was clearly trading on past glories to a certain extent. So long as big-name stars were keen to play alongside a hero from the past – and perhaps gain a little "credibility" in the process – and record buyers were content to hear retreads of his old classics, he couldn't lose. What's remarkable, however, is how satisfying the latter-day Hooker albums really are, and how much energy and commitment he continues to bring to the recording studio.

Mr Lucky, the 1991 follow-up to *The Healer*, is the best of the lot. This time around, the project was bursting with big names, all male (Bonnie Raitt had been a welcome presence on *The Healer*) and all eager to show off their chops. With the exception of **Backstabbers**, however, which is drowned beneath Albert Collins' searing Texas guitar, it's unmistakably a John Lee Hooker record throughout. On the opening track, **I Want To Hug You**, the rollicking boogie of Chuck Berry's longtime pianist Johnnie Johnson incites Hooker into a swaggering, confident mood that barely lets up thereafter. Later on, Keith Richards turns up to tangle guitars on a memorable **Crawling King Snake**, and Van Morrison duets on **I Cover The Waterfront**, complete with a churchy organ overdub from Booker T. Jones.

Two of the most enjoyable ensemble pieces are the rumbustious **This Is Hip** – the one that dissolves into a chant of "That's a rocking good way" – cut with Ry Cooder and the members of his short-lived supergroup Little Village, and the jazz-tinged **Stripped Me Naked**, a bitter monologue about Hooker's divorce. Carlos Santana, who wrote the music with his band, returns to play guitar, while Hooker supplies the vocals, which include a gloriously atmospheric rant about the "mean old judge".

If you still need convincing that John Lee Hooker can still deliver the downhome Delta blues, head straight for the two predominantly acoustic tracks, on which he's accompanied by John Hammond on slide guitar and harmonica. **Father Was A Jockey** is a boogie-ing Mississippian slice of sexual bragging, a switchback ride between brooding menace and roaring exultation adorned with the trademark Hooker stomp, and the six-minute **Highway 13** finds John Lee in even better voice as he drives through the rain trying to find his baby.

➲ We almost chose **The Healer**, Silvertone, 1989

28

Lightnin' Hopkins

Mojo Hand

Rhino, 1993; recorded 1946–69

Although Lightnin' Hopkins is generally seen as a solo maverick from the lone-star state, he had an awful lot in common with John Lee Hooker. Like Hooker, he began his career in the late 1940s purveying his own personal brand of electric boogie, and never abandoned his trademark rhythms even when recast as an acoustic troubadour during the 1960s. Also like Hooker, his disdain for formal musical structures made it hard to work with others, but he could produce such a full and complex sound on his own that it barely mattered. Finally, he shared Hooker's willingness to record for anyone and everyone who'd pay him upfront. Hopkins was so prolific during the 1960s that it wasn't unusual for him to record three albums in a week, and with dozens of those albums still available it's difficult to know where to start. It's not even a question of simply buying his greatest hits: "po' Lightnin'" never really had any.

Fortunately, Rhino's twin-CD **Mojo Hand** compilation serves as a magnificent overview of a career that ranged through gospel, zydeco and early rock'n'roll, as well as blues. It offers glimpses of Hopkins playing piano and organ as well as guitar, and working in a duo or with small jazz bands as well as alone. The first track, **Blues Is A Feeling**, spotlights Lightnin' as he's probably best remembered, in genial live performance at a hootenanny in 1962; the remaining forty tracks are in chronological order and tell a more complex story of his remarkable life.

The die was cast for young Sam Hopkins, of Centerville,

Texas, when at the age of 8, in 1920, he was introduced to Blind Lemon Jefferson. Hopkins had just made his first guitar and, with Jefferson's blessing, was a hobo-ing musician himself within a few years. Sam became Lightnin' in 1946, when Aladdin Records packed him off to Los Angeles to record alongside pianist Wilson "Thunder" Smith. Both his first two singles, Katie Mae Blues and Tampa Red's Play With Your Poodle, were local hits in Texas, but although Lightnin' cut forty more sides for Aladdin he wasn't interested in pursuing stardom. Instead, he was happy to reel off effortlessly memorable discs like Baby Please Don't Go and Short Haired Woman for Houston label Gold Star at $100 a time.

During the early 1950s, Hopkins enjoyed national R&B hits on the Sittin' In With label with Give Me Central 209 and Coffee Blues. Sadly, his chart run ended just as he made perhaps the finest records of his career. Herald releases like 1954's Movin' On Out Boogie now sound way ahead of their time, their infectious metronomic boogie crackling with energy. By the time researcher Samuel Charters located him in Houston in 1959, Hopkins had reverted to being a minor local celebrity. Charters taped an album for Folkways in Hopkins' hotel room that "introduced him to the modern intellectual audience for the blues." Fan It provides a taste of the new acoustic Lightnin', as later heard on Arhoolie Records, among others.

Despite achieving, and relishing, international renown in his later years, Hopkins did more than simply plough the same old groove. Among enjoyable off-the-wall moments preserved here are Shaggy Dad from 1965, a strange little number on which he's accompanied by Earl Palmer on drums and John Ewing on trombone, and Los Angeles Boogie from 1969, which finds him pumping enthusiastically at the organ. Even his reworkings of much-visited themes were consistently fresh and inventive, as on Mojo Hand itself, cut for Arhoolie in 1969, and the two-part Mr Charlie from the same year. He died in comfortable retirement in Houston in 1982.

⮞ We almost chose **The Herald Recordings 1954 Vol.1**, Collectables, 1991

29

Son House

Preachin' The Blues

Catfish, 2000; recorded 1930–42

Eddie "Son" House seems forever doomed to be remembered more for his connections than for his own achievements. When folklorist Alan Lomax interviewed House in the Delta in 1941, he was ecstatic at finding the "missing link" between Blind Lemon Jefferson and Robert Johnson. Similarly, when House was "rediscovered" in 1964, eager blues students quizzed him endlessly about Johnson and Charlie Patton rather than about himself. It is true that, unlike his contemporary, Skip James, Son House was not so much a unique original as firmly placed in the heart of the Delta blues tradition. That doesn't mean that the awesome power of his music deserves to be neglected. By compiling the cream of his early recordings onto the cut-price seventy-minute CD, **Preachin' The Blues**, Catfish have done blues fans everywhere a great service.

Son House is generally regarded as having been born in the Delta in 1902, though he also referred to 1885 as being his birth date. He came from a religious family, and in his youth was vehemently opposed to the blues: "I just hated to see a guy with a guitar. I was so churchy!". He even became a preacher and, long after his distaste for plantation work – and taste for liquor – turned him towards music in the late 1920s, the tension between God and the Devil remained. He told Lomax that he'd learned to play guitar in Clarksdale from a man who owned all Blind Lemon Jefferson's records and that he in turn had taught Robert Johnson the little he knew.

In 1930, not long after Jefferson's death, Paramount Records invited Charlie Patton, their biggest surviving blues star, to bring a group of Delta musicians to his next recording session in Wisconsin. Patton rounded up both Son and another new acquaintance, Willie Brown, and they all drove north. *Preachin' The Blues* opens with an extraordinary test acetate of Walking Blues, discovered in 1985, which seems to have been cut as a rehearsal piece. It's eye-opening stuff, with House slashing at his slide guitar while Brown boogies on second guitar and someone vamps away on harmonica. Surely a glimpse of what really went on in the juke joints of the Delta, it sounds like Chicago blues twenty years before its time. The three two-part slide-guitar classics on which Son House's reputation originally rested then follow: My Black Mama, Dry Spell Blues, and the seminal Preachin' The Blues, in which House claims he "met the blues this morning walking just like a man."

While House was exultant at receiving forty dollars for that session – "it'd take me near about a whole year to make forty dollars in the cotton patch" – his records didn't sell. He continued to perform on the juke-joint circuit, however, in tandem with Willie Brown, and his first thought when Lomax came calling in 1941 was to rope Brown in too. Lomax was to recall that "of all my times with the blues, this was the best one"; House remembered: "all I got was a bottle of Coke, but it was cold and good." Thirteen tracks here come either from that trip or Lomax's return visit in 1942. Highlights include two versions of Charlie Patton's signature tune, Pony Blues; a clutch of searingly personal songs such as County Farm Blues and Low Down Dirty Dog Blues; and the bizarre waltz-time American Defense, a meditation on the US entry into World War II.

Though House "retired" from playing the blues after Brown's death in 1952, he was able during the 1960s, with a little prompting, to recapture his old intensity and produce several worthwhile albums. By his own reckoning, he was over 100 years old when he died, in Detroit in 1988.

➲ We almost chose **The Friends Of Charlie Patton**, Yazoo, 1998

30

Howlin' Wolf

Howlin' Wolf / Moanin' In The Moonlight

MCA, 1987; recorded 1951–61

Imagine every ingredient that went into creating the blues – all the rage and passion of the Mississippi Delta, all the electric thunder and urgency of Chicago – compressed within a single mighty frame, and bursting to be released. Even to his contemporaries, Howlin' Wolf seemed more of an elemental force than a flesh-and-blood human being. Crawling across the stage on all fours, baying like a wounded animal, roaring out his pain and pride, he was the most essential bluesman of them all. No one has ever surpassed the magnificence of the music collected on his first two Chess albums, now available on a single cut-price CD as **Howlin' Wolf/Moanin' In The Moonlight**.

The Wolf began life in West Point, Mississippi, in 1910, as Chester Arthur Burnett. At the age of 13, he moved with his family to Dockery's plantation outside Clarksdale. He was taught guitar by none other than Charlie Patton and later learned harmonica from Sonny Boy Williamson II, who was briefly his brother-in-law. Never more than minimally competent on either instrument, he was still doggedly taking lessons at over 60. He was unable to read or write and could barely even count enough to keep formal time. What he did have was perhaps the most awesome singing voice ever recorded, imbued with a ferocious authority and power yet suffused with vulnerability and despair. His gruffness owed much to Patton, while his ululating howl was drawn from examples like Tommy Johnson, the Mississippi Sheiks, and especially country pioneer Jimmie Rodgers, the

"Singing Brakeman": "I couldn't do no yodellin', so I turned to growlin', then howlin', and it's done me fine."

Though he performed all over Mississippi with the likes of Sonny Boy and Robert Johnson, Wolf remained a farmer until he moved to Memphis when he was 38. There he became a DJ, and formed a band with Junior Parker on harp and Willie Johnson (not the blind one) on guitar. Spotted by Ike Turner, he cut **Moanin' At Midnight** and **How Many More Years** for Sam Phillips' Memphis Recording Service in 1951. Even before Johnson's angry distorted guitar could kick in, the primeval howl of the Wolf demanded to be heard. Phillips later regretted that he "would have loved to have recorded that man until the day he died", but the discs were such a success when leased to Chess that the label persuaded Wolf to sign an exclusive contract and move north.

Although Wolf was a cantankerous collaborator even at the best of times, his subsequent career benefited from the input of some superb sidemen. Hubert Sumlin's devastating razor-edge guitar work was a vital component of masterpieces like **Smokestack Lightnin'** and **The Red Rooster** (based on Patton's "Moon Going Down" and "Banty Rooster" respectively). In live performances, and on his early recordings, Wolf repeatedly reworked songs from his youth, as when he recycled a Tommy Johnson motif on **I Asked For Water (She Gave Me Gasoline)**.

As the years went by, the songwriting skills of Willie Dixon added breadth and depth to his repertoire; among the ten tracks tailored to Wolf's personality that feature here are **Little Baby**, **Back Door Man** and **Spoonful**. Nonetheless, Wolf saw Chess' insistence that he record Dixon's songs as a plot to deprive him of royalties. He loathed **Wang Dang Doodle** in particular, and memorably described Dixon as "that fat fuck" in an interview. Ultimately, however, the baleful presence of the Wolf, bristling with menace on the likes of **Evil** and **Forty Four**, dominates everything he recorded. This CD represents only a small fraction of his output, which continued until his death in 1976, but it's as overwhelming an experience as the blues has to offer.

➲ We almost chose **His Best**, Chess, 1997

31

Mississippi John Hurt

Avalon Blues

Columbia, 1996; recorded 1928

During the folk revival of the 1960s, record companies rushed to recast hard-bitten purveyors of gritty urban blues as acoustic troubadours. Of all the heroes of the folk-blues scene, none was a more genuine folk musician than Mississippi John Hurt. What seduced those earnest students who "rediscovered" Hurt in 1963 were his lyrical renditions of traditional songs and ballads. Cut during his one previous brush with the music industry in 1928, these classic accounts are now collected on **Avalon Blues**. Such material would have sounded old when first recorded, so when Hurt re-emerged, at the age of 70, still performing in the same timeless style, he seemed a direct link with the roots of American popular music.

Born in Teoc, Mississippi, in 1893, Hurt taught himself guitar from the age of 9. His repertoire was therefore amassed before the blues even had a name. For the next sixty years, his life centered on the tiny Delta village of Avalon, near Greenwood. Working on the railroad, on the river, and especially on local farms, his contact with other musicians was minimal. As a result, he evolved a distinctive playing technique, using three fingers and no picks to produce a rolling, mellifluous guitar sound with an undercurrent of syncopated rhythm that owed much to ragtime.

Hurt's first recordings were made for the OKeh label in Memphis in February 1928. The only titles ever released from that initial session, **Frankie** and **Nobody's Dirty Business**, are the first two tracks on *Avalon Blues*. "Frankie", a saga of betrayal and murder known elsewhere as "Frankie And Albert" (and later, as in the Sam Cooke hit, as "Frankie And Johnny"), exists in over three hundred versions in the Library of Congress. Hurt's performance is regarded as definitive more for the beauty of his picking than the coherence of the story. There's little narrative thrust; we know that Frankie shoots Albert, because "he was her man, but he was doing her wrong", but not what happens at her trial, while a stray verse is tacked onto the end, out of sequence. Hurt's gentle delivery contrasts oddly with the gory subject, as it does again in "Nobody's Dirty Business", an equally pleasant melody in which he states "one of these days gonna wake up boozy, gonna grab my gun, gonna kill old Suzie."

Later in 1928, OKeh invited Hurt to record again in New York, stipulating that he include at least four "old time tunes". In the most memorable, Stack O'Lee, pretty finger-picking and lilting vocals once more deliver a tale of cold-blooded slaughter. The original Stacker (or Stagger) Lee, who killed a man over a Stetson hat, may have been a Mississippi steamboat owner or his mulatto bastard son. Greil Marcus has traced his career as a folk villain through Jamaican rude boys to the Clash's tribute on *London Calling* in 1980. Here, too, Hurt seems rather uncertain of the words, but the overall effect is irresistible.

The one truly personal piece Hurt recorded in 1928 was Avalon Blues itself, on which he laments being in New York rather than Avalon, "my home town, always on my mind." His eagerness to go home may have owed something to the sessions taking place either side of Christmas. In any case, this was the song that made his 1960s re-emergence possible; blues enthusiasts simply made their way to Avalon and were directed to his house from the local gas station. Hurt subsequently enjoyed a three-year Indian summer as a recording artist and performer on the festival and coffee-house circuit before his death in 1966.

➲ We almost chose **Complete Works 1927–29**, Document, 1990

32

Papa Charlie Jackson

Complete Recorded Works Vol.1

Document, 1994; recorded 1924–26

Though Papa Charlie Jackson was not the first solo male blues performer ever to be recorded – that distinction belongs to Sylvester Weaver – he was certainly the first to have any commercial impact. The initial volume of his **Complete Recorded Works**, which covers his first 27 sides from August 1924 up to February 1926, is therefore a major historical document. It is also a highly enjoyable record in its own right, and with repeated listenings makes you realize just how much of the range, depth, sophistication and joy of the blues was there from the very beginning. The one drawback is the substandard sound quality, despite a fair stab at cleaning up Paramount's dreadful tapes.

Born in New Orleans around 1885, Jackson learned his craft in the travelling medicine shows of the South. The nature of his music as a bridge between old-time vaudeville and the nascent blues is encapsulated by the instrument he played: the banjo-guitar, in which six guitar strings acquired a jaunty sound through being laid across the body of a banjo. Gus Cannon was the only other significant exponent of this hybrid, which could be tuned to different chords for each song.

When he came to the attention of Paramount Records in the early 1920s, Jackson was living in Chicago. Perhaps unsurprisingly, the company had little idea whether a market for blues records even existed. A 1927 promotional booklet recalled scepticism that "no one wanted to hear comedy songs sung by a man strumming a banjo." Soon enough, however, "Charlie . . . took the entire country by storm, and now – people like nothing better than to come home after a tiring and busy day and play his records."

In truth, those early trailblazers still have an irresistible charm. As shown by both sides of his first release – **Papa's Lawdy Lawdy Blues** and **Airy Man Blues** (which should be "hairy man") – Jackson had a great ear for a catchy chorus, while his deadpan tone in announcing "I got a wife, got a girl, and I'm fooling on the outside too" has remained a blues trademark to this day. His first genuine hit, the sprightly **Shake That Thing**, from May 1925, was also the first blues dance hit, and ranks as the forerunner of countless variations on the "Shake 'Em On Down" and "Rollin' And Tumblin'" themes.

Even if Jackson can't claim to have composed them, several blues classics make their first appearances here. During the delightful **I'm Alabama Bound**, which had already been published several times, he mentions "Elder Green", about whom Charlie Patton later sang to the same tune. Patton also picked up **All I Want Is A Spoonful**, passing it in turn to Howlin' Wolf and on to Cream. **Shave 'Em Dry**, which here consists of a string of innocuous unrelated verses, was subsequently transformed by Lucille Bogan into possibly the filthiest blues ever recorded.

Songs that Jackson probably did write, on the other hand, include **Salt Lake City Blues**, a string of Mormon jokes given extra power by the unstated fact that blacks were at the time not welcome in Utah, and **Jackson's Blues**, celebrating a black civil rights champion in Chicago. The CD also includes three duets with Ida Cox, including a fascinating stop-go version of **How Long Daddy, How Long**.

Papa Charlie was to remain in Chicago for the rest of his life. As well as recording with Blind Blake, he's said to have taught Big Bill Broonzy to play the guitar, and made some unreleased recordings with him in 1935. His own career, however, tailed off during the Depression, and his death in 1938 went largely unnoticed.

⊃ We almost chose **Fat Mouth**, Yazoo, 1991

33

Elmore James

The Sky Is Crying: The History Of Elmore James

Rhino, 1993; recorded 1951–61

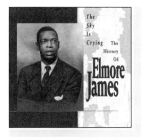

As perhaps the first man to realize what a racket you can make with an electric guitar, Elmore James has got an awful lot to answer for. His blistering riffs have been the model for almost every blues-rock behemoth on the planet for nigh on four decades. He also inspired some truly dreadful singers who mistook his pent-up, at times quasi-hysterical, vocal style as license to shout their way through the entire Robert Johnson songbook. It's always a welcome shock, therefore, to rediscover just how wonderful his own catalogue really is.

There's no better opportunity to do so than Rhino's 23-track compilation, **The Sky Is Crying**. Drawing on his work for eight different labels, it displays a much greater range of abilities than is commonly imagined, and shows his lesser-known material as entirely worthy of standing along his acknowledged classics.

Born in 1918 in Richland, Mississippi, he learned his music in the Delta in the 1930s. After wartime service in the Pacific, he acquired his first electric guitar around 1945, and seized upon its potential to create entirely new sounds. In particular, he adapted traditional slide or bottleneck techniques to the new technology, learning to control and relish the distortions that came from attacking his strings with a piece of metal pipe. On top of that, his skill as a radio repairman stood him in good stead when it came to cranking every last drop of juice out of his amplifiers.

As a regular on Sonny Boy Williamson's King Biscuit Time radio show, James broadcast his discoveries across the Delta. He was not recorded, however, until the tail end of Sonny Boy's second session for Trumpet Records, in Jackson, Mississippi, in 1951. Contrary to a much-repeated legend, James was fully aware that he was being recorded, and set out his stall with magnificent deliberation. Dust My Broom remains a seminal moment in blues history, with James launching full tilt into that unforgettable riff and Sonny Boy Williamson II answering him right back with his harp. Though James had learned the song from Robert Johnson, it went back further than that. The actual phrase "I believe I'll dust my broom" was first heard on record on Kokomo Arnold's "Sagefield Woman Blues". James didn't even record a B-side, but the cut was a Top Ten R&B hit.

James bought a car with his royalties, and he needed it. Racing around the country, and swiftly establishing a reputation on the club scene in Chicago, he recorded for a quick-fire succession of labels. Often all they wanted was a "Dust My Broom" retread, but given the chance he was equally adept at slow, searing blues ballads. Most of the time, he was backed by Tampa Red's former band, who as the Broomdusters included "Homesick James" Williamson on rhythm guitar, Johnny Jones on piano, and Odie Payne on drums. The crucial factor on tracks like The Sky Is Crying, It Hurts Me Too, Madison Blues and Hawaiian Boogie, however, lies in the ongoing "conversation" between James' guitar and J.T. Brown's tenor sax. James didn't always play slide; beautiful examples of his fingered style include My Best Friend and the 1960 version of Rollin' And Tumblin'.

Further jewels spilling from the Elmore James treasure chest include definitive versions of I Can't Hold Out, Look On Yonder Wall, Standing At The Crossroads and Shake Your Moneymaker, with Joe Turner's original James-backed T V Mama thrown in for good measure. James himself didn't live to see their elevation to the blues pantheon. Old before his time, thanks to a chronic heart condition, he died aged 45 in Chicago in May 1963.

➲ We almost chose Let's Cut It, Emd/Virgin, 1987

34

Etta James

Her Best

Chess, 1997; recorded 1960–73

As her consistently earth-shattering vocal performances on the twenty-track compilation **Her Best** amply demonstrate, Etta James ranks among the greatest of all blues singers. Many of her biggest hits date from the early 1960s, just before soul music took shape, when the devastating power of a gospel-schooled voice was so often set against poppy, swing-tinged string arrangements. Etta didn't so much transcend such surroundings as transform them, to create gritty blues classics that were also pop gems.

Half black, half Italian, Etta James was born Jamesetta Hawkins in Los Angeles in January 1938. By the age of 5, she was singing on air with her local church choir. She was "discovered" at 16, when she auditioned for bandleader Johnny Otis, together with two friends, as the Peaches (Etta's nickname). Their "Roll With Me, Henry", a riposte to Hank Ballard's "Work With Me, Annie", was a national hit under the sanitized title of "The Wallflower", and young Etta embarked on a nonstop cavalcade of cross-country touring.

By the time she came to Chess in 1960, grace of her connection with Harvey Fuqua of the Moonglows, the 22-year-old Etta was a grizzled veteran alarmed by her waning chart status. Even as the frail teenager pictured on the sleeve of *Her Best*, complete with dyed-blonde cropped hair, she had sung with an adult power and passion. Label owner Leonard Chess was determined to harness that intensity and make her a star. Etta may have resented his crude methods – "when I would get to a part where he thought I should squawl or scream 'wheeawow!' he'd punch me in the side. I mean literally *punch* me" – but they worked. In the space of three years, she notched up ten hits on both the R&B and pop charts.

From the moment you hear the languid string introduction to the first track, At Last, you know this isn't going to be your standard Chess blues. Then Etta comes in with a gloriously drawn out "At last . . .", and sweeps you away. Her first Chess chart success, All I Could Do Is Cry, written by Berry and Gwen Gordy, points towards Motown, with Etta anticipating the young Diana Ross. Similar 1960 ballads included A Sunday Kind Of Love and My Dearest Darling.

Only one of James' duets with Fuqua – himself later a Motown stalwart – features here. The smouldering If I Can't Have You is a meaty enough blues-based piece but less effective than its obvious inspiration, Jimmy Reed's Baby What You Want Me To Do. Etta's solo live rendition of the latter, recorded in Nashville in 1963, is a bravura triumph, as she growls and purrs to an audience that's eating out of her hand.

James' finest hour, however, came at Rick Hall's Fame Studios in Muscle Shoals in 1967. The aim was to capture the new horn-driven "Deep Soul" sound, and the shadow of Aretha clearly lay over the proceedings, but she certainly did the business. The smash hit was her classic take on Clarence Carter's Tell Mama, but she also came up with a cut of Otis Redding's Security that outsold Otis, and the show-stopping I'd Rather Go Blind.

Though plagued by personal and drug-related problems, Etta James stayed at Chess until 1975. After a subdued 1980s, she re-emerged in strong form in the 1990s, issuing such new material as a set of Billie Holiday songs and duetting with B.B. King. There's much more to her than her Chess catalogue, but if you're looking for a belting blues workout *Her Best* makes the perfect place to start.

⮑ We almost chose **Etta James Rocks The House**, Chess, 1992

35

Skip James

The Complete Early Recordings

Yazoo, 1994; recorded 1931

If ever the blues has boasted a true tortured genius, that man was Skip James. No one else has mastered both guitar and piano to the same degree, nor combined the two with talents as singer and composer to produce such haunting, transcendentally beautiful music. Paradoxically, the very fact that James didn't disappear into history but instead lived long enough to be "rediscovered" in the 1960s, may be the thing that prevented him from being considered as the greatest blues artist of them all.

By the standards of his Mississippi contemporaries, Nehemiah Curtis James had a privileged upbringing. The son of a Baptist preacher, he was born in Bentonia near Yazoo City, south of the Delta, in 1902. His nickname dates from his high-school days, when he was known as "Skippy" on account of his dancing style. Claims that he typifies a "Bentonia school" of the blues are wishful thinking: James was very much a one-off, a highly proficient instrumentalist whose own self-belief ran in tandem with despair at the world. Exposure to fiddle-driven dance music around 1910 inspired him to take up the guitar. His later remark that "I wondered what the blues was then" suggests a sense of childhood innocence; certainly the adult Skip became imbued with a very dark sensibility indeed.

The one recording session of James' youth, collected on **The Complete Early Recordings**, took place at the Paramount studios in Grafton, Wisconsin, in February 1931 (not 1930, as the CD cover states). Things kicks off with the stunning **Devil Got My Woman**. The song had featured in his repertoire even before his 16-year-old wife left him, but the sheer personal intensity of "I'd rather be the devil, than be that woman's man" goes way beyond artifice. It's a clear prefiguration of Robert Johnson's doom-laden "Hellhound On My Trail", not least because of James's haunting high tenor.

A similar spiritual malaise permeates **Cypress Grove Blues** – "I would rather be buried in some cypress grove, than to have some woman that I can't control." James wrote the song in the cypress grove beside the Big Black River where he cut his timber, and it's the preacher's boy's agonized conviction that "you got to reap just what you sow" that gives the song its chilling strength. Another genuine classic, **I'm So Glad**, is a virtuoso guitar piece, so fast that some experts have called it "impossible" to play. Despite the title, and its origins as a children's song, "I'm So Glad" oozes pain and weariness: "I'm tired of weeping, tired of moaning, tired of groaning for you."

Eleven of James' thirteen guitar performances here are played in "cross-note" tuning (E-B-E-G-B-E), which he learned from a neighbour who'd picked it up in turn from Bahamian soldiers in France during World War I. The style of his five piano pieces, in contrast, is his alone. Stabbing out staccato phrases, often with a single hand, and stamping his feet to add percussion, he verges on the brink of frenzy. **22–20 Blues**, which he claimed to have improvised in the three minutes it took to record, was later all but copied by Robert Johnson as "32–20 Blues".

The Depression meant that James's record sales were too low to fulfil his ambition of escaping "a strainy livin'" and, with his early dreams dashed and the fact that Paramount went broke owing him money, he came to regard the music business as a "barrel of crabs". Nevertheless, these 1931 recordings – grainy, faded, bristling with angst – stand as his greatest achievement and one of blues' finest monuments.

➲ We almost chose **Complete Recorded Works 1931**, Document, 1994

36

Skip James

Today!

Vanguard, 1989; recorded 1966

Devotees of the blues love to insist that it's fundamentally a music of redemption and joy, and bemoan its popular image as being obsessed with misery and woe. But if tears in your eyes and a lump in your throat is what you want, there can be few sadder artists in any medium than Nehemiah "Skip" James. He may have been an unlovable misanthrope, but if anyone ever captured the sound of a soul in torment, Skip did.

Skip James was all but unique among those bluesmen "rediscovered" in the 1960s in remaining capable of building on the legacy of his eerily majestic 1931 recordings (see p.69). Life had not been kind to him in the intervening years. Following spells as both a Baptist and a Methodist preacher, he recast himself as "a common ordinary Skip", and was working as a plantation labourer when eager students found him in the spring 1964, suffering from undiagnosed syphilis in a Tunica County hospital bed. Within weeks, he was performing to great acclaim at the Newport Folk Festival.

The best of the albums Skip went on to record before his death in 1969 was his second for the Vanguard label, **Today!**. Cut in 1966, at the tail end of the blues revival, it was not a commercial success, but although at least seven of its twelve tracks are re-makes of his 1931 masterpieces – the precise count depends on whether you consider All Night Long as identical to "If You Haven't Any Hay" – it's no mere retread of past glories. In place of the desperate flamboyance of his youth, his guitar playing is now characterized by a studious precision; his piano seduces rather than assaults, while his singing is imbued with a mordant introspection. James claimed that the music he played in the 1960s came from his head, whereas in the 1930s it had come from his heart. If he'd lost his faith in the blues along with his faith in God, he hadn't lost his faith in his own genius.

Hard Times Killing Floor Blues, with which *Today!* opens, is a meticulous, definitive rendition of the one early song in which James looked beyond his own circumstances to contemplate the tribulations of his peers. Written at the start of the Depression, it's now sung with self-assured maturity by an old man who knows he's created a classic.

James crystal-clear falsetto is heard at its best on the almost unbearably poignant **Washington D.C. Hospital Center Blues**, a new song commemorating the kindness he'd received after wellwishers arranged his transfer to the capital. Few concrete details emerge beyond his eagerness to convince both them and himself that he deserved such treatment: "I was a good man, but I was a poor man."

Cypress Grove also receives a considered reappraisal, while only on **I'm So Glad** does he conspicuously fail to match his earlier technical proficiency. As James himself commented of the rock group Cream's hit version, "it's too good a song to mess up like that." **Crow Jane** and **Drunken Spree** both reproduce the sound of the pre-blues dance pieces on which Skip was raised.

Ultimately Skip James' reputation will always rest on his youthful brilliance, when his intensity and conviction made him more compelling even than Robert Johnson. *Today!* makes less painful listening – not least because of the advances in recording technology – while also being an exquisite and deeply moving document of a great artist given one final chance to set out his stall.

➲ We almost chose **Devil Got My Woman**, Vanguard, 1989

37

Blind Lemon Jefferson

Squeeze My Lemon

Catfish, 1999; recorded 1926–29

Blind Lemon Jefferson has been called the first superstar of the blues. If that sounds extreme, consider a sermon released after Jefferson froze to death in a Chicago snowstorm in 1930, in which Reverend Emmet Dickinson opined that his life was "in many respects like that of our Lord Jesus Christ. Like Him, unto the age of 30 he was unknown, And also like Him, in a short space of a little over three years, His name and his works were known in every home." Before Jefferson, almost all blues records had been made by women singers. He was not literally the first male country blues singer to be captured on disc, but without his stupendous sales the genre might have withered on the vine, and he can therefore take credit for the very existence of much of the music celebrated in this book. He himself cut around 86 tracks in those three years, 23 of which are collected on Catfish's budget compilation **Squeeze My Lemon**.

Born as the youngest of seven children near Couchman, Texas, in 1897, Jefferson was nicknamed "Lemon" because he was a chubby child. Though blind from birth, his only known photo shows him wearing wire-framed spectacles, and is signed "Cordially yours, Blind Lemon Jefferson." Playing for tips on the streets of Dallas, led around by such future luminaries as Leadbelly and T-Bone Walker, he made a decent enough living to buy his own car and employ a chauffeur. Unusually, he even earned considerable royalties from his records.

After being spotted by talent scouts in Texas, Jefferson was taken to Chicago by Paramount Records in the winter of 1925/26. Uncertain whether there was a demand for his brand of intense rural blues, the company marketed his debut release as "a real, old fashioned blues, by a real, old fashioned blues singer." But such songs as the gambling saga Jack O'Diamond Blues and Chock House Blues tapped into a previously unsuspected audience.

Some see Jefferson as having established a distinct style of "Texas blues", but he was in many ways too idiosyncratic a performer to inspire direct copyists. He seldom stuck for long to the standard interplay of answering each vocal line with a corresponding guitar phrase; instead, each time he drew breath his restless fingers seemed to improvise their own separate narrative, and if it took a few extra beats for them to get where he wanted to go, so be it.

His greatest significance lies in the raw personal intensity of his finest songs. Black Snake Moan, from 1927, is particularly staggering. Hailed by Paramount as "weird, slimy, and creepy", it was based on a Victoria Spivey song that really was about a snake. In Jefferson's hands, however, the "black snake crawlin' in my room" is something very different. The sexual urgency in his voice is among many moments here that presage rock'n'roll; he even sings "that's all right mama, that's all right for you." There's another Elvis echo in "the train I ride, eighteen coaches long", on Right Of Way Blues, while Matchbox Blues was itself a hit for Carl Perkins at Sun and was later recorded by the Beatles.

That Crawling Baby Blues, from Jefferson's final 1929 session, is a disturbing tale of paranoia and emotional turmoil: "many man rocks some other man's baby and the fool thinks he's rocking his own." For guaranteed shivers down the spine, however, try See That My Grave Is Kept Clean, a variation of the traditional "Two White Horses In A Line", in which he foresees his own death, complete with the tolling of the church bell at the funeral.

➲ We almost chose **King Of The Country Blues**, Yazoo, 1990

38

Little Willie John

All 15 Of His Chart Hits

King, 1996; recorded 1955–61

Little Willie John is one of those seminal figures of 1950s R&B who, because they're so hard to pigeonhole, end up falling between the cracks. His chart heyday was over by the time soul came along, so he never became a soul star himself. In the end, though, it doesn't matter who he influenced, or what he might have done in his own right if life had worked out differently. The records he did make are just *so* good, and above all there's that fabulous, once-heard-never-forgotten voice. The reason he's included here is that he started out singing blues ballads, and he sang them as sublimely as it's possible to imagine. So well, in fact, that however far he subsequently strayed from the genre, everything he touched remained imbued with the blues.

Though born in Arkansas in 1937, William Edward John was raised in Detroit. One of ten siblings – the eldest, Mable, recorded for both Motown and Stax in the 1960s – he learned to sing in church, and his parents were appalled when he turned his talents to secular music. By the age of 13, he was winning talent contests at Detroit's Paradise Theater, singing with Dizzy Gillespie's band. At 16, contracted to Syd Nathan's King Records, he was on the road. A mere fifteen years later he was dead, from pneumonia contracted while serving time for manslaughter.

All 15 Of His Chart Hits collects the stream of R&B and pop smashes that started in 1955, when Little Willie John was still only 17. Look at a photo of him when he was recording this stuff, and you see a slight, happy-go-lucky teenager just five foot two inches tall. Listen to the records, however, and you hear not only a mature and utterly intense adult voice, but also an awesome frightening pain and passion. The despair in these sagas of loss and loneliness is overwhelming. Despite few overt gospel tricks – just a slight choking at the end of specific lines – the effect is both purer and rawer than even a superb singer like Sam Cooke ever achieved and, if anything, Little Willie John was at his grittiest at the very start of his career.

John's first hit, **All Around The World**, was an R&B number written by Titus Turner, and later revived by Little Milton as "Grits Ain't Groceries". Apart from a robust saxophone blast, John carries the song with bravura confidence. Follow-up **I Need Your Love So Bad** is an unquestionable blues classic, written by Willie's brother Mertis John. Peter Green's Fleetwood Mac and Buddy Guy have recorded it since, but no one has the tortured conviction of Little Willie as he begs, "I need someone to tell me when I'm lyin'."

Fever, up next, tops everything. John's snappy, sassy, but at the same time heart-rendingly compelling rendition, was his biggest success. Although Peggy Lee's subsequent pale imitation only sold half as many copies, sadly it's her version that's always remembered in the pop history books.

While the rest of the CD doesn't quite maintain the exalted standard of those three opening tracks, there's plenty more to enjoy. The most unambiguous pleasures are the slow ballads **Let Them Talk**, **Now You Know** and **Talk To Me, Talk To Me**, and the faster-paced **Take My Love (I Want To Give It All To You)**, also by Mertis John, which provided Little Willie's last chart entry in 1961. Elsewhere, even when you can't help smiling at the cheesy arrangements – check out the strings on **The Very Thought Of You**, the organ on **Sleep**, or the mewling on **Leave My Kitten Alone** – John's magnificent singing will never let you down.

> ➲ We almost chose **Fever: The Best Of Little Willie John**, Rhino, 1993

39

Blind Willie Johnson

The Complete Blind Willie Johnson

Columbia, 1993; recorded 1927–30

Despite the fact that he didn't actually play the blues, the Texas evangelist Blind Willie Johnson has long been accepted as a sort of honorary bluesman. That's largely thanks to his unparalleled abilities as a slide guitarist, although, once you get over the initial shock, there's also something irresistible about the overwhelming leonine bellow of his voice.

Part wandering preacher, part street musician, Johnson was a musician with a repertoire restricted to hymns, gospel tunes and moralistic ballads, and yet, at his peak he managed to outsell Bessie Smith. All thirty sides he ever recorded, between 1927 and 1930, have been collected and restored on **The Complete Willie Johnson** and they're still guaranteed to send shivers down the spine. During the 1960s blues revival, many of his posthumous champions assumed he had written his own material; at the time, however, his songs were largely familiar from church. Hence his repeated use of his guitar as a substitute for his voice – with the words already known, he often sang only half of each line, completing the phrase on the guitar instead.

Johnson was born in Temple, Texas, some time between 1890 and 1902, and moved as a baby to Marlin, south of Dallas. He first picked up a guitar and expressed his ambition to be a preacher at the age of 5; he was blinded when his stepmother threw lye in his face two years later. By the time he came to record, in Dallas in December 1927, he was a sublimely accomplished slide guitarist, who could wring every nuance from a melody as he pressed down on the strings with the blade of his pocketknife. Those sessions produced a passionate rendition of **Motherless Children Have A Hard Time**, but are best remembered for the extraordinary free-form **Dark Was The Night, Cold Was The Ground**, an almost wordless piece in which his mournful slide is backed only by meditative humming and the odd exclamation of "well" or "lord". For Johnson, the message was more important than his own virtuosity, so on this and future dates he also switched to the much cruder, heavily percussive picking technique displayed on songs such as **If I Had My Way I'd Tear That Building Down**. An oft-told story tells how he was arrested outside the Custom House in New Orleans for singing this latter, though in fact it's about Samson and Delilah.

On each of Johnson's three further studio visits – Dallas in 1928, New Orleans in 1929, and Atlanta in 1930 – he was accompanied by a female singer. In Dallas and Atlanta, his wife Willie Harris provided appealing harmonies and also completed some of his lines for him, adding an extra element to the blend of wailing slide and growling voice. In New Orleans, an anonymous churchwoman simply chipped in whenever she happened to know the words. Highlights from those sessions include overtly religious songs, like **Praise God I'm Satisfied**, as well as the topical ballads he probably bought as sheet music from street evangelists. **Jesus Is Coming Soon** describes the recent "Spanishin' flu" epidemic, when the people were "dyin' on account of their wicked ways"; **When The War Was On** recounts popular experience of the Great War; and **God Moves On The Water** is typical of a then-popular genre that saw the sinking of the *Titanic* as evidence of divine retribution.

When his career was ended by the downturn in record sales during the Depression, Johnson returned to poverty and obscurity in Beaumont, Texas. He died in 1947 when he caught pneumonia after his shack burned down, and was confined to bed with only damp newspapers for blankets.

➲ We almost chose **Praise God I'm Satisfied**, Yazoo, 1991

40

Lonnie Johnson

Steppin' On The Blues

Columbia, 1990; recorded 1925–32

Singer-guitarist Lonnie Johnson is unique among the great bluesmen in having been equally at home playing either blues or jazz – indeed, he had a significant role in inventing both. During the hectic first flourish of a prolific recording career that was to last over forty years, he cut country-blues masterpieces that paved the way for Robert Johnson, and fiery jazz instrumentals that inspired Django Reinhardt. Perversely, his very proficiency may have damaged his reputation, in that an ability to play in any style to order is hardly a hallmark of the "authentic" roots musician. **Steppin' On The Blues** makes a powerful case for Johnson as a true giant of the blues, presenting prime examples of both his blues and jazz work, as well as much more besides, all beautifully restored to pristine clarity.

Raised in New Orleans around the turn of the twentieth century, Alonzo Johnson was exposed to all the myriad musical influences that have shaped popular music ever since. Starting out on the violin, he also learned banjo, mandolin and piano before he settled on the guitar. He's often credited with inventing the "guitar solo", as an improvised stream of notes interjected mid-song, suggested perhaps in part by his own experience on the violin and also by the horn sound of his hometown.

Johnson's earliest professional engagements were in the clubs of New Orleans' legendary red-light district, Storyville, though he played on tour in London as early as 1917. After losing his family in the postwar influenza epidemic, he relocated to St

Louis, where he performed on steamboats with Charlie Creath's Jazz-O-Maniacs. At the tail end of his debut recording session with the group, in 1925, he cut a disc under his own name, **Mr Johnson's Blues**. Not until he won a talent show held at the city's Booker T. Washington Theater, however, did OKeh Records invite him to sign a contract as a blues artist.

During the seven years covered by *Steppin' On The Blues*, Johnson recorded around two hundred sides, and enjoyed tremendous sales. His biggest hit, the folk standard "Careless Love" from 1928, is not included here, but songs like **Mean Old Bedbug Blues** and **No More Trouble Blues** were widely circulated and much covered. He also accompanied other artists, whether playing guitar behind the old-fashioned hollers of Texas Alexander, as on **No More Women Blues** and **Deep Blue Sea Blues**, or duetting as a singer with Victoria Spivey on ribald numbers such as **Toothache Blues**. Robert Johnson was so taken with Lonnie Johnson's early recordings that he adopted not only his vocal and guitar stylings but even his name, and is said to have passed himself off as a cousin.

Even within Lonnie Johnson's blues material – and despite his own comment that "I recorded 125 songs against the same chords" – there's a great deal of lyrical and structural complexity. **She's Making Whoopee In Hell Tonight** and **Got The Blues For Murder Only** are both intricate self-penned elaborations of the traditional blues format. The most impressive pieces here, however, are the more jazz-tinged tracks. There's nothing from the sessions he cut with either Louis Armstrong or Duke Ellington, but the two duets he made in 1928 with white jazz guitarist Eddie Lang (who hid behind the pseudonym Blind Willie Dunn) boast an astonishing sophistication and fluency. Both **Guitar Blues** and **Have To Change Keys (To Play These Blues)** eerily anticipate the work of Charlie Christian, T-Bone Walker and B.B. King. The solo instrumentals, too – like the Django-esque **Playing With The Strings** and the previously unissued 1927 master here called **Untitled** – are every bit as dazzling.

➲ We almost chose **He's A Jelly Roll Baker**, Bluebird, 1992

41

Lonnie Johnson

Blues & Ballads

Bluesville, 1990; recorded 1960

Though Lonnie Johnson's life in the blues had its highs and lows, his awesome skills enabled him to ride the storms and retain his integrity all the way from the 1920s until his death in 1970. His early heyday as a recording artist, commemorated on *Steppin' On The Blues* (see p.79), came to an end with the Depression. Five years later Johnson began another successful run with Lester Melrose's Bluebird label in Chicago, and was hailed by poet Langston Hughes as the "finest living male singer of the Blues." After this, he moved to Cincinnati, where his 1948 waxing of the ballad "Tomorrow Night" for King Records was a #1 R&B hit, and was subsequently covered by, among others, Elvis Presley.

Blues & Ballads dates from the final phase of Johnson's career. By the end of the 1950s, his star had begun to wane, and he was forced to work as a janitor in a hotel in Philadelphia. "Rediscovered" by radio DJ Chris Albertson, he recorded a succession of albums for the Bluesville subsidiary of Prestige Records. These in turn triggered a return to live performing on the festival circuit that was only ended by his death in 1969 following a car accident. For the second of his Bluesville albums, *Blues & Ballads*, he was teamed up with a close contemporary, guitarist and banjoist Elmer Snowden. The two men, with occasional accompaniment from Wendell Marshall on bass, were let loose in a New Jersey studio to record whatever they felt like – the results were a delight.

By now into his sixties (at the very least), Johnson was much mellower and more contemplative than he had been as a youth, but neither age nor the switch to playing an electric guitar had dimmed his technical excellence. As for Snowden – whose original claim to fame was that he'd founded a band in 1921 that was eventually taken over by its pianist, Duke Ellington – it was his first opportunity to record since 1934.

Johnson's horizons always extended far beyond the blues, and in his later years he was especially interested in exploring his abilities as a crooner. On his many appearances on the coffee-house and festival circuit during the 1960s blues revival, he'd regularly perform swinging big-band numbers. While the basic plan with *Blues & Ballads* was to produce a blues album, once in the studio Johnson launched into a stream of tear-jerking ballads. His most powerful vocal performances were on two of his own songs, opening track Haunted House and the gloriously sentimental love song I Found A Dream. The even more lazily seductive standard Memories of You was embellished with a particularly tasteful guitar solo.

Tackling more traditional blues pieces, Johnson displayed his old improvisational flair, turning W.C. Handy's chestnut St Louis Blues into a snazzy rhumba, complete with Spanish-scented intro. He also revisited a couple of his own staples, in the shape of Back Water Blues, a Bessie Smith tune he'd first recorded in 1927, and signature song Jelly Roll Baker, a saucy little number bursting with double entendres that he'd cut for Bluebird in 1942. Snowden got his own chance to stretch out on a couple of gorgeous instrumentals: the delicate five-minute Blues For Chris and the much more upfront boogie-ing Elmer's Blues, on which Johnson exhorts him to ever greater heights all the way through.

Blues & Ballads is a rare and splendid opportunity to hear two master musicians with nothing left to prove playing the music they love for pleasure. As such, it is also as life-affirming a blues album as you could ever hope to find.

➲ We almost chose **Me And My Crazy Self**, Charly, 1992

42

Robert Johnson

The Complete Recordings

Columbia, 1990; recorded 1936–37

Robert Johnson is universally acknowledged as the most important figure in blues history. In two brief recording sessions, he both produced the definitive consummation of the prewar acoustic "country blues" of the South, and established a blueprint for the urbanized and electrified blues of the North. That he died young and virtually unrecognized – a death presaged in the doom-laden intensity of his finest material – made him the archetypal romantic bluesman.

When his music first became widely known, during the 1960s, Robert Johnson remained a man of mystery. His raw artistry seemed beyond tradition, and blues fans eagerly told how he had acquired it through a Faustian pact, selling his soul to the Devil at a lonely Delta crossroads.

Born in May 1911, in Hazelhurst, Mississippi, Johnson was the eleventh child of Julia Dodds, although not fathered by her husband Charles. As an adult, he wandered as far afield as Chicago, New York and Canada supporting himself by playing at rent parties, in juke joints, or on the street. A widower at 19 when his 16-year-old wife died in childbirth, Johnson's inveterate womanizing eventually brought him down. He died in Greenwood, Mississippi, on August 16, 1938, after drinking poisoned whisky given him by a juke-joint proprietor who resented Johnson's obvious interest in his wife.

Columbia's lavish two-CD box set presents **The Complete Recordings** – 41 sides produced at San Antonio in November

1936 and Dallas in June 1937. They appear here in precise chronological order, which means listening to back-to-back versions of those twelve songs for which he recorded alternate takes.

In subjecting Johnson's musical roots to the same scrutiny as his family history, historians have stripped away much of the myth. Many of his lyrics, and also his vocal and musical mannerisms, were borrowed from the recordings of Kokomo Arnold, Lonnie Johnson, Charlie Patton and Son House. Johnson stands revealed as not so much an unschooled original as the first modern blues performer, with a genius for synthesizing others' raw material into something uniquely his own.

The songs on which Johnson's reputation rests – such as **Hellhound On My Trail**, **Me And The Devil Blues** and **Come On In My Kitchen** – are imbued with a real sense of despair. They reveal Johnson as a soul in torment, at times desperately fleeing the forces of evil, and, at others in league with the Devil. Neither he, nor the women he both mistreats and idolizes, understands the demon that drives him towards self-destruction. "You may bury my body down by the highway side/So that my old evil spirit can get a Greyhound bus and ride." These songs are no less personal for using long-standard blues couplets or guitar figures. Neither does it matter whether their conviction owes more to Johnson's professional skills than any genuine distress. The "real" Robert Johnson may be the one displayed in the exuberant double entendres of **Terraplane Blues** – "When I mash down on your little starter/Then your spark plug will give me fire" – which was by far his most successful recording.

Regarding Robert Johnson as primarily a sensitive singer-songwriter also ignores the fact that his most lasting influence was in his music rather than his lyrics. **Sweet Home Chicago** became an anthem for Chicago bluesmen not because of its words – which are largely gibberish with no relevance to Chicago – but because its combination of insistent rhythmic boogie-ing on the bass-line with simultaneous fingered embellishments laid down a template for the future of amplified blues.

➲ We almost chose **King Of The Delta Blues**, Sony, 1999

43

Tommy Johnson

Tommy Johnson & Associates

Catfish, 1999; recorded 1928–35

One of the most original performers of the early Delta blues, Tommy Johnson has never quite received the respect he deserves. Although he long outlived both Charlie Patton and Robert Johnson, his self-destructive nature ensured that his recorded legacy was far smaller – just a handful of finely crafted songs stand as his monument. As a guitarist, Johnson was perhaps too skilful for his own good, in that he devised exquisitely appropriate accompaniments for each piece rather than playing in a consistently characteristic style. His voice, however, is unique: clear and melodious for the most part, and thus more readily understandable today than most of his peers, he'd often slip for emotional effect into an eerie and unforgettable falsetto. That quasi-yodel was later echoed by the first star of country music, Jimmie Rodgers.

The Catfish compilation, **Tommy Johnson & Associates**, preserves the most important eight of the fourteen sides Johnson ever cut, along with fourteen relevant tracks by his contemporaries. As well as placing Johnson clearly in context, it's a great listen in its own right, holding some truly beautiful music.

Born the son of a former slave in Terry, Mississippi, in 1896, during early adulthood Johnson gravitated to the Dockery Plantation on the edge of the Delta. Although he already played rudimentary guitar, his musical horizons were expanded at the Dockery Plantation. He was the first bluesman to spread the story that he'd learned his art after selling his soul to the Devil at a crossroads; in truth he did the next best thing, teaming up with such seminal figures as Charlie Patton and Willie Brown.

From the 1920s onwards, Johnson based himself in Jackson, where his house became a way station for black musicians. Around 1926, he auditioned for store owner and recording scout H.C. Speir, and was told to come back when he knew more than one song. He duly returned two years later with four solid-gold classics.

The compelling **Big Road Blues** was Johnson's tour de force, resting on his mournful cry that "I ain't going down that big road by myself." Author David Evans wrote an entire book about its enduring influence, not only in terms of its lyrics but also in the piano-like "walking bass" of Johnson's guitar. Among remakes featured on this CD are the Mississippi Sheiks' **Stop And Listen Blues**, with its lead fiddle and reference to "smoke-stack lightning, shines like gold"; Kokomo Arnold's **Stop Look And Listen**; and Bumble Bee Slim's **Sad And Lonesome** and **Rough Road Blues**.

Cool Drink Of Water Blues – "I asked her for water, she give me gasoline" – was eventually the prototype for another Howlin' Wolf song, "I Asked For Water", and Wolf's roar can be traced back to Johnson's more querulous howl. Ishmon Bracey's own heavily percussive **Saturday Blues**, recorded at the same session with Johnson on guitar, used the same "I asked for water" refrain. Musicologists debate whether Johnson or Patton wrote the tune that Tommy called **Bye-Bye Blues**, and which Patton cut a year later as his signature piece, "Pony Blues".

The sadly prophetic **Canned Heat Blues** – which gave its name to the 1960s blues-rock group – refers to Johnson's addiction to alcohol in any available form, be it shoe polish or paint stripper. Although he managed four more sides in 1928, when Paramount invited him to Wisconsin in 1929 he was too drunk to record more than six songs in two weeks, and even on those his powers were sadly in decline. It was another 27 years before he finally went down the big road by himself, however; he died in 1956 while performing at a Saturday-night house party.

➲ We almost chose **Complete Recorded Works**, Document, 1994

44

Junior Kimbrough

Sad Days Lonely Nights

Fat Possum, 1998; recorded 1993

Sad Days Lonely Nights

Junior Kimbrough and the Soul Blues Boys

When David "Junior" Kimbrough first came to public attention from his home in Mississippi's hill country, thanks to Robert Palmer's 1992 movie documentary *Deep Blues*, he was hailed as a sort of primitive original, a kind of "bluesman that time forgot". If that gives you any preconceptions as to what he might sound like, they're almost certainly wrong. Neither nimble-fingered guitar-picker nor Delta bottleneck stylist – let alone sensitive, wounded poet of the blues – Kimbrough worked in a little-known tradition that was to some extent of his own devising. If anything, he was way ahead of the rest of the music world and, despite his preceding Elvis, it took the emergence of grunge for him to strike a chord with the record-buying public. The closest analogy for rock-attuned ears is probably latter-day Neil Young, as recorded live with Crazy Horse.

Although Kimbrough worked as a garage mechanic throughout his adult life, he was playing in the juke joints of northern Mississippi by the time he was 20, in 1950, and continued to do so for fifty years until his death in 1998. Sun rockabilly pioneer Charlie Feathers, who encountered him in those early years, recalled him as "the beginning and the end of music". A couple of 1960s forays into recording studios produced three or four occasionally anthologized tracks, but Kimbrough's was essentially a live music. Critic Robert Palmer first came across him in Kimbrough's own juke joint, housed in a former church in

Chulahoma, ten miles west of Holly Springs. That was the setting for his first, Palmer-produced CD for the Fat Possum label, 1992's acclaimed *All Night Long*, and was used again the following year for **Sad Days Lonely Nights**.

There's little to choose between the two albums. Both were recorded in what amounted to live conditions, with each song cut in a single take and no subsequent overdubs. The precise personnel of the "Soul Blues Boys" varies, but is drawn either from Kimbrough's extended family or that of his longtime neighbour, playing companion and labelmate R.L. Burnside. Burnside's son Garry plays bass on both, while *Sad Days Lonely Nights* also features Cedrick Jackson on drums plus an additional guitarist, Kenny Brown, to provide extra beef. It's also fifteen minutes longer, its eleven tracks stretching to 65 minutes. Since a long, drawn-out groove is what Junior's blues are all about, that's as good a reason as any to call it essential.

As Kimbrough told one interviewer, "my songs, they have just the one chord, there's none of that fancy stuff you hear now, with lots of chords in one song. If I find another chord I leave it for another song." Even to call them songs is pushing it. Most are in the same key, you can hardly make out a word he sings, and it's hard to tell where one ends and the next begins. All are credited to Kimbrough, except the traditional Old Black Mattie – an R.L. Burnside staple – and John Lee Hooker's Crawling King Snake, and that's so unrecognizable there was no real need to acknowledge Hooker.

We're left, therefore, with a compelling, extended, thrashed-out boogie, which it's easy to imagine would go on all night if only Kimbrough had the same space on record as he did live. It makes an intriguing companion piece to R.L. Burnside's own *Come On In* (see p.15). Here, the tapes were simply left to roll, while on Burnside's they were spliced, looped, deconstructed and reassembled; and yet the overall trance-like effect is ultimately very similar, with a relentless repetition that's endlessly fascinating and never palls.

➲ We almost chose **All Night Long**, Fat Possum, 1997

45

Albert King

King Of The Blues Guitar

Atlantic, 1989; recorded 1966–68

During ten glorious years, from the early 1960s onwards, Memphis-based Stax Records was *the* soul-music label, carrying artists like Otis Redding and Isaac Hayes to huge international success. Of the small roster of blues performers that the label maintained as a sideline, only Albert King made an even vaguely similar impact. However, the albums he recorded for Stax are not only the best of his career, but also the most satisfying blues-soul hybrids ever created. That's not to belittle the blues-imbued soul balladeering of singers like Bobby Bland or Z.Z. Hill; it's just that King boasted such a pure, driving and utterly distinctive blues guitar sound that he could hold his own in any company. He may have stretched the definition of the blues, but in doing so he simply made it bigger and better.

Albert King was born Albert Nelson near Indianola, Mississippi, in April 1923. Indianola was also the birthplace of B.B. King, whose surname he appropriated soon after B.B. came to fame. Based in Gary, Indiana, during the early 1950s, Albert King played drums behind Jimmy Reed and cut a handful of solo singles for Parrot in Chicago. He then moved to St Louis, where the Bobbin label gave him a national R&B hit in 1961 with "Don't Throw Your Love On Me So Strong".

King remained a minor figure, however, until 1966, when he persuaded Stax founder Estelle Axton to take a chance on the blues. The audition piece she suggested, Laundromat Blues, was an immediate hit, and was followed up by a steady stream of well-received singles, plus an even more influential LP, *Born Under A Bad Sign*. **King Of The Blues Guitar** was originally a separate album, but as a CD reissue it incorporates the whole of *Born Under A Bad Sign*, making it the definitive collection of King's 1960s Stax output.

By the time he reached Stax, King's own guitar style was firmly defined. His unique sound, at once crackling with energy but somehow supremely languid, owed much to his playing his "Flying V" Gibson left-handed. That he did so without re-stringing the instrument effectively precluded him from playing most conventional chords; instead he relied on fluid single-note runs.

His great good fortune at Stax was to benefit from the astounding work rate of the label's in-house musicians. Despite being premier-league hit-makers in their own right, Booker T. and the MGs backed King on every track of **King Of The Blues Guitar**. All deserve full credit, as do the Memphis Horns, but the real jewel in King's crown was Al Jackson – later the mainstay of Al Green's phenomenal Hi recordings – who, in addition to his own rock-solid, ever-inventive drumming, handled most of the production chores. Though King's playing made him a darling of the West Coast psychedelic scene, through regular appearances at San Francisco's Fillmore Auditorium, the rock trappings never made him lose sight of his blues roots.

Almost every cut here is irresistible, but the real highlight is Born Under A Bad Sign itself, King's definitive lament that "If it wasn't for bad luck, you know I wouldn't have no luck at all." His solo was promptly lifted by Eric Clapton, among others, but never surpassed. The downhome rendition of Crosscut Saw, first recorded by Tommy McLennan in 1941, was another instant classic. Cold Feet and Funk-Shun were two funky self-penned jams. Among the ballads, Ivory Joe Hunter's I Almost Lost My Mind features some lovely interplay with the horns, while As The Years Go Passing By is a loving pastiche of Bobby Bland's 1950s sound graced by another exquisite solo.

➲ We almost chose **The Ultimate Collection**, Rhino, 1993

Albert King

I Wanna Get Funky

Stax, 1990; recorded 1972

Albert King's first Stax recordings, as collected on *King Of The Blues Guitar*, are generally considered his finest work. However, his final Stax album, **I Wanna Get Funky**, recorded in 1972 and released in 1974, in many ways represents a more intriguing exploration of the blues-soul hinterland. The studio was rapidly approaching the end of its world-beating run, and with Booker T. and the MGs no longer available King was backed instead by their successors the Bar-Kays. From the very start of this album, both musicians and production are on top form. King isn't asked to carry the tunes; instead he pours his cranked-up "Flying V" guitar all over the trademark Stax mix – a tight foundation of fatback bass and drums punctuated by short, sharp phrases from the Memphis Horns. Extra depth and texture is added, at appropriate moments, by the Memphis Symphony Orchestra.

One of Albert King's many borrowings from his namesake B.B. King was to name his guitar "Lucy", in honour of B.B's "Lucille". King's identification of his instrumental sound with a woman's voice seems at its most plausible on this album. There's a striking contrast throughout between King's laid-back, barely articulated vocal style and the piercing, crystal-clear notes that flow from his guitar. On several tracks, he doesn't so much sing as ruminate to himself. Flat Tire consists of a monologue in which he searches for someone to help him fix a flat while his baby is left stewing in the car. The sense of disconnection is even played for laughs when his backing vocalists, Hot Buttered Soul, mishear what he's singing.

'Til My Back Ain't Got No Bone is an even more extended funk workout. For several minutes, King muses as to what he'll say to his baby when he finds a phone, and then mumbles through assorted wrong numbers and crossed lines. Just when he seems trapped in Barry White territory, his guitar finally bursts through and takes over.

The clearest summation of what getting funky was all about comes on the reworked eight-minute take of **Crosscut Saw**, when King exhorts the band to "do it like we used to do it, back in 1965." Having meticulously reproduced the pared-down sound of the tight little combo with whom he first recorded the song, he launches into a much less disciplined, but far more exuberant, guitar solo that truly puts the fun into funky.

Walking The Back Streets And Crying is another tour de force. Recorded by Little Milton in the same year (as a straight, impassioned blues ballad), in King's hands it's an ambivalent, confused but ultimately inspiring masterpiece, in which his guitar explicitly represents the voice of the central female figure. **Playing On Me**, written by Stax staffer Mack Rice, is more conventional in its soul-man posturing, but there are further powerful personal testimonies in the elegiac **I Can't Hear Nothing But The Blues**, in which King asserts his individuality while paying tribute to his parents, and the snappy **Travelin' Man**. Proceedings draw to a close with the anthemic **That's What The Blues Is All About**, which sees King consciously asserting his customary persona as just an ordinary Joe – although as he told one interviewer, "I wouldn't be here today if it had all happened to me."

After Stax folded, King pursued the funk down to New Orleans, recording the great "Angel Of Mercy" single with Allen Toussaint and the Meters. Although he remained a tremendous live performer until his death in 1992, his work on album was never again so consistently inspired.

➲ We almost chose **King Does The King's Things**, Stax, 1990

47

B.B. King

Singin' The Blues / The Blues

Flair, 1993; recorded 1951–61

For most of the fifty years since his first hit record, the name of B.B. King has been synonymous with the blues. A stream of albums, and even more prodigious schedule of live appearances, has made him the world's favourite bluesman – a true ambassador of the blues. While keeping faith with the purists, he's consistently grown and developed as an artist, and has helped to change the shape of the music itself. The reason he's so hard to characterize as belonging to any specific subgenre of the blues is that he has transcended them all, and many modern guitarists who think of themselves as simply playing "the blues" are in fact following a pathway that B.B. originally trod alone.

The cream of the 1950s recordings that put B.B. on the map were originally gathered on his first two albums, now available as a single CD, **Singin' The Blues / The Blues** – the perfect introduction to his work. Although his technical proficiency has never stopped improving, these two albums show the essential components of his style already firmly in place.

Riley King was born in Mississippi, between Itta Bena and Indianola, in September 1925. A highly unsettled childhood meant that by the age of 9 he was living alone and working as a tenant farmer. His first exposure to music came through singing in church, though he also heard Sonny Boy Williamson I and other great Delta figures. After a brief wartime spell in the army, life as a musician seemed preferable to driving tractors, and he began performing for tips with gospel quartets on Memphis' legendary Beale

Street. Having failed to master the Delta tradition of slide (or "bottleneck") guitar – despite tuition from his cousin Bukka White – he turned instead to jazzmen like Django Reinhardt and Charlie Christian for inspiration. Hearing T-Bone Walker bring similar single-string techniques to the blues on "Stormy Monday" in 1947 persuaded him to buy his first electric guitar.

Both King's guitar playing and his singing shared a supple fluency. On guitar, he'd hit slightly off the desired note and then either slide his fingers or push and "bend" the strings until he reached it. In the same way, his pure gospel voice would glide from one note to the next, often pausing within a single syllable to sustain a high note before resuming its onward flow. He was always hesitant about playing chords to accompany himself, let alone anyone else; instead, in classic blues tradition, his guitar lines complemented his vocal delivery, even down to being echoed by his famous facial grimaces.

King's stint presenting the Sepia Swing Club on the first all-black radio station in the US – WDIA, the "Mother Station of the Negroes" – led to a session for Nashville-based Bullet Records in 1949. Those early sides barely featured his guitar, and his real breakthrough came two years later in Memphis, where he cut Three O'Clock Blues for LA's Modern label. Playing impassioned lead over an almost ponderous rhythm section of two saxes, piano and drums, he completely overshadowed Lowell Fulson's 1948 version of the song.

For the rest of the 1950s, the hits came thick and fast. Every Day (I Have The Blues), a Memphis Slim original, had also been popularized by Lowell Fulson, while Sweet Little Angel hymned the same "sweet black angel" previously celebrated by Robert Nighthawk and Tampa Red. Slow ballads like You Know I Love You tended to provide King's biggest sellers, but he was becoming more and more adept at a kind of energetic free-form improvisation displayed on That Ain't The Way To Do It, Troubles, Troubles, Troubles and Don't You Want A Man Like Me.

➲ We almost chose **His Definitive Greatest Hits**, Universal Music TV, 1999

48

B.B. King

Live At The Regal

Beat Goes On, 1997; recorded 1964

As if being regarded as the definitive live blues album of all time were not enough, **Live At The Regal** also marks a pivotal moment not only in B.B. King's own personal history but also for the blues as a whole. By the time King arrived for a week-long residency at Chicago's Regal Theater in November 1964, he had established himself through ceaseless touring as the biggest star on the so-called "chitlin'" circuit of black entertainment venues. He'd yet to make any significant inroads with the white market, however, and his record company, ABC-Paramount, who had signed him in 1961 in the hope of emulating the crossover success they'd previously enjoyed with Ray Charles, were starting to worry. After all, black audiences were themselves deserting the blues in favour of the more contemporary and more politicized sound of soul, as epitomized by James Brown and Otis Redding.

Wisely, ABC decided to return to basics, and record King on his chosen domain, doing what he did best – playing in front of his devoted fans. King's studio recordings had always been characterized by the way his singing voice would take over where his guitar left off and vice versa. Taping a live performance added another voice to the mix – that of the audience. Even in 1964 there were few black theatres left where King could be guaranteed the kind of responsive crowd he needed. The Regal fitted the bill to perfection and the interplay between audience and star is one of the principal joys of the resultant album.

The B.B. King captured on *Live At The Regal* was not yet the elder statesman so familiar today. Still in his thirties, his voice sounded young, even if he was already straining to reach the high notes of his early years. On guitar, the exuberance of his attack on uptempo numbers like Please Love Me and Woke Up This Mornin' was that of an energetic adult in his prime. Though King himself was never an out-and-out speed merchant, this was the album that caught the imaginations of would-be blues-rockers the world over, and in doing so triggered his move into the rock auditorium and festival circuit.

Live At The Regal was programmed to reproduce the experience of being in the actual theatre. On CD, it still includes the DJ introductions to the "world's greatest blues singer" that kicked off each side of the original album, as well as plenty of spoken narrative from B.B. himself. As ever, his opening number is Memphis Slim's Every Day (I Have The Blues); he's been quoted elsewhere as saying "I always start my show with [it] because it's true." Atop the steady riffing of his three-man horn section and the galloping drums of Sonny Freeman, King races into action, spewing wildfire flurries from his guitar amid his ecstatic gospel vocals. The pace then immediately drops for a stately rendition of Sweet Little Angel, propelled through all its verses by the piano of Duke Jethro and climaxing when King unleashes his guitar, the legendary Lucille, into an inspired, less-is-more solo.

The rest of the album continued to intersperse faster and slower songs with both King and Lucille providing a running commentary throughout. King had clearly worked with the band long enough for them to follow his every cue; this enables him to toy with the tempos and manipulate audience expectations. Particular highlights include Worry, Worry, which boasts a brace of stunning solos, and the deceptively smooth ballad with which the album closes, Charlie Singleton's Help The Poor, in which the "poor" in question is actually "poor me".

➲ We almost chose **Blues Is King**, MCA, 1990

49

B.B. King

Indianola Mississippi Seeds

MCA, 1989; recorded 1970

Only six years passed between the 1964 Chicago concert commemorated on *Live At The Regal* (see p.95) and the Los Angeles sessions that resulted in **Indianola Mississippi Seeds**, but for B. B. King everything had changed. Once he'd imagined he'd play out his life performing to mostly black audiences; now he was appearing before capacity crowds not only in the US but all over the world. He was finally getting his just rewards, to the extent of claiming back his copyrights on all those 1950s songs whose credits had been assigned to fictitious names like "Taub", "Josea" and "Ling". ABC Records had stuck with him, creating the Bluesway imprint to showcase his new releases and even given him his first Top 20 pop hit with "The Thrill Is Gone" from the 1969 album *Completely Well*.

Indianola Mississippi Seeds, the follow-up, was produced by Bill Szymczyk, the man responsible for adding strings to "The Thrill", a step that has always appalled certain blues purists. Perhaps surrounding B.B. King with a bevy of Johnny-come-lately rock stars doesn't sound all that promising on paper, but the result is nothing like all those ego-laden superstar jams of the period, and King himself always said that "*Indianola Mississippi Seeds* was the best album I've done artistically." Above all – a simple but obvious stratagem – the only lead guitar comes from the man himself. Three of the nine tracks do feature a rhythm guitarist – in two instances, it's Joe Walsh of

Eagles fame – but otherwise the guitar is only heard when Lucille chooses to speak. Part of the idea of framing B.B. King in a "rock" setting was no doubt to let him show all his blues-rock copyists that he was still the boss, but typically enough he achieved that through taste, timing and restraint rather than blistering fretwork.

What's especially likable about *Indianola Mississippi Seeds* is that it's playful rather than po-faced, always exploring and experimenting. A defining moment comes when Chains And Things suddenly changes direction three-quarters of the way through. B.B. hit a wrong note but was going so well he kept playing anyway. After he dug his way out, he added a matching burst of strings to make his mistake seem deliberate. A similar sense of fun pervades the guitar–piano dialogues between King on Lucille and either Carole King or Leon Russell on keyboards. Carole King, in particular, is a revelation, trading licks with her namesake while allowing him space to manoeuvre.

The album opens with B.B. alone at the piano for a one-verse snatch of the jokey Nobody Loves Me But My Mother ("and she could be jivin' too"). That segues straight into his guitar intro for the superb six-minute You're Still My Woman, on which the roomy arrangement enables Lucille to soar at will before the strings finally enter and sweep it all away. Ain't Gonna Worry My Life Anymore comes the closest to repeating that magic, thanks again in part to Carole King, and here too the triumphant mood of the strings is surely tongue-in-cheek. King's Special, too, is a gem, in which he mimics a steam train as it gathers momentum, then chugs at full steam ahead before finally pulling peacefully into the station.

Undeniably, *Indianola Mississippi Seeds* does have its weaker aspects – not least the cheesy sleeve depicting a watermelon dolled up as a guitar, the generally clodhopping drums, and the "angelic chorus" that rounds off Hummingbird – but it's an enjoyable and exhilàrating glimpse of B.B. King at his very best. Who could ask for more?

➲ We almost chose **Together Live: B.B. King & Bobby Bland**, MCA, 1987

50

Freddy King

Hideaway

Blues Encore, 1996; recorded 1956–68

As if there weren't enough "Kings" in the blues already, there were at least two Freddy Kings. OK, so both were contained within the same mighty six foot seven inch frame, but while one reeled off light, poppy, dazzlingly fluent instrumentals, the other squeezed out heartfelt, gritty masterpieces of urban blues. During his lifetime, his albums tended to focus on one aspect or other, so only on the compilations released since his premature death in 1976 has it been possible to appreciate both sides of his personality. **Hideaway** – issued by the budget European label Blues Encore (and chosen here in preference to the similar, identically named Rhino anthology on grounds of price) – contains a superb selection of the tracks on which his reputation rests.

Born in Texas in 1934, and raised listening to the likes of Lightnin' Hopkins, he moved as a teenager to Chicago. The family home being behind the legendary *Club Zanzibar*, young Freddy used to sneak in to watch Muddy Waters performing with Jimmy Rogers. They taught him to play guitar using picks on both finger and thumb. King soon formed his own band, and the limited local success of his 1956 debut single for El Bee records, coupling Country Boy with That's What You Think, was enough to make him leave his job in a steelworks and turn pro. Despite a stellar line-up of musicians, including Billy "The Kid" Emerson on piano, and Robert Lockwood on guitar, neither song is now especially interesting, while King's vocals are disappointingly diffident.

In 1960, however, talent scout and pianist Sonny Thompson took King to Cincinnati, where he signed to the Federal label, a subsidiary of King Records. Things happened fast: on his first day in the studio, King recorded five stone-cold classics. The first to be released, the ballad You've Got To Love Her With A Feeling, was a small-scale hit, but it was the follow-up, Hideaway, that made Freddy's name. A dynamic instrumental, it was based in part on a warm-up theme he'd performed while working with Hound Dog Taylor, and in part on Jimmy McCracklin's "The Walk". In the US, it climbed the pop charts as a fun, frivolous beach-party anthem; in the UK, on the other hand, it was received with reverence, and mastering its supple, flowing lines became a rite of passage for British blues guitarists. It was Eric Clapton's signature tune with John Mayall's Bluesbreakers, and Clapton went on to champion Freddy for the rest of his life. Another King song, Have You Ever Loved A Woman, provided a key moment on his album *Layla*.

Meanwhile, Freddy found himself cast in America as an honorary Californian beach bum. His albums were given titles like *Freddie King Goes Surfin'*, and he even cut something called "The Bossa Nova Watusi Twist". Nonetheless, the music still sounds great. Highlights among the exhilarating instrumentals on *Hideaway* include The Stumble, San-Ho-Zay, and the reverb-drenched Sen-Sa-Shun. As rock guitarists later in the 1960s came to appreciate, all could basically be dropped into the middle of other songs to serve as solos. Here, in their original form and devoid of any rock-god pretension, they're bursting with freshly minted glee and innocence.

Following further vocal triumphs from the Federal years, such as Someday, After A While (You'll Be Sorry) and (The Welfare) Turns Its Back On You, *Hideaway* closes with a gem from King's subsequent spell with Atlantic – Let Me Down Easy, featuring composer King Curtis on sax and James Booker on piano.

⮞ We almost chose **Hideaway**, Rhino, 1993

51

Leadbelly

King Of The 12-String Guitar

Columbia, 1991; recorded 1935

There are two great anomalies about Huddie "Leadbelly" Ledbetter. The first is that he remains such a familiar figure despite having died over fifty years ago. The second is that his fame has endured despite his having had such minimal impact on black audiences or fellow performers either in his lifetime or since. **King Of The 12-String Guitar** collects the fruits of one of his few attempts to appeal to black record buyers, an attempt that was so unsuccessful that most were not even released during his lifetime. Now lovingly restored as part of Columbia's excellent Legacy series of reissues, however, they provide the best available insight into the man and his music.

Were it not supported by prison archives, the saga of Leadbelly might seem too archetypal to be true. Born around 1890, he was raised on his parents' farm in western Louisiana, close to the Texas border. Though music was a family tradition, he wasn't exposed to the blues until he started to make solo forays to the nearest large town, Shreveport. During early adulthood in Texas, he's said to have worked as Blind Lemon Jefferson's "lead man", and acquired both his first twelve-string guitar and an ear-to-ear scar. Sentenced to thirty years' imprisonment for murdering a man in 1917, he "sang his way out" by writing a song to Texas' state governor pleading for a pardon, which he duly received in 1925. Five years later he was back in prison for assault, this time in Louisiana's infamous Angola Penitentiary.

It was there that he was "discovered" by folklorist John A. Lomax in 1934. Searching for songs rather than singers, Lomax concentrated on prisons, on the basis that men serving long sentences would be "uncontaminated" by newer material. In Leadbelly, he swiftly recognized that he'd hit the mother lode. Huddie was a true "songster", who combined an extraordinary repertoire of songs and styles with a compelling physical presence as a performer. Amazingly, he "sang his way out" again, when a similar plea to the governor of Louisiana, recorded and delivered by Lomax, brought quick results.

In a relationship that to modern sensibilities seems questionable to say the least, the newly freed Leadbelly went into Lomax's service, and headed north. As well as acting as Lomax's driver and talent scout, Leadbelly appeared on stage as a sort of living example during his lectures on folklore – at times posing in striped prison uniform to add an extra frisson – and also shared copyright on the songs the two men published. Leadbelly became a celebrity, lionized in *Life* magazine under the headline "Bad Nigger Makes Good Minstrel" and featuring on the *March Of Time* newsreel.

The recordings on *King Of The 12-String Guitar* date from the start of Leadbelly's new career, barely six months after his release from prison. His best-remembered work, such as "Rock Island Line" and the song that in other hands became "Goodnight, Irene", was cut later for the archives of the Library of Congress, but the aim here was strictly commercial. Although hollers such as Honey, I'm All Out And Down and work songs like Ox Drivin' Blues sounded dated to contemporary black audiences, that is in a sense what makes them so intriguing today. The CD now serves as a one-man overview of the black music scene, both popular and traditional, of almost a century ago. If you're used to the later, more overtly "folk" Leadbelly, it's a surprise to hear him playing slide guitar on Packin' Trunk, while the bass runs on the two-part Roberta exemplify what early Texas blues was all about.

➲ We almost chose **Where Did You Sleep Last Night**, Folkways, 1996

52

J.B. Lenoir

His JOB Recordings

Paula, 1991; recorded 1951–54

It would be nice to imagine that, were it not for his untimely death as a result of a car crash in 1967, J.B. Lenoir would now rank as a major star. Sadly, however, he ploughed a lonely furrow during his lifetime, never achieving significant sales even during his lengthy 1950s' sojourn with Chess, and there's little to suggest his luck was about to change. If Lenoir is remembered at all, it's as one of the few Chicago bluesmen who put the lie to Samuel Charter's famous assertion that "there is little social protest in the blues." When a strong CD compilation of his Chess works becomes readily available, it'll count as an essential purchase. For the moment, however, this book settles instead for two red-hot collections from either end of his career, with **His JOB Recordings** serving to show where it all began.

Lenoir was a Depression-era child of the Deep South, born in 1929 in Monticello, southern Mississippi. That's much closer to Louisiana than the Delta, which explains the surname, though he pronounced it "Lenore" rather than with a French intonation. Strangely enough, J.B. was his actual Christian name, not his initials. As he later recalled, both his father and brother "used to play nothin' but blues", styling themselves especially on Blind Lemon Jefferson. J.B. himself gravitated to New Orleans in adolescence, where he's said to have linked up with Elmore James and Sonny Boy Williamson II, before moving north to Chicago in 1949.

If J.B.'s role model down south was Lightnin' Hopkins, once up north he seems to have come under the spell of John Lee Hooker and Jimmy Reed. Which is to say he loved to boogie, accompanying his steady riffing with unusually high-pitched vocals. According to Willie Dixon, the young Lenoir "was a helluva showman, 'cause he had this long tiger-striped coat with tails" – though the one he's wearing on the CD sleeve looks more like a zebra-skin tux. He came to the attention of Joe Brown, owner of JOB Records, in 1951, but his first track, "Korea Blues", was leased to Chess and is unfortunately missing here.

For JOB, Lenoir started out recording with his own small-scale live band, the Bayou Boys, which consisted of Sunnyland Slim on piano and Alfred Wallace on drums. His debut release on the label, **Let's Roll**, a powerhouse boogie propelled by both guitar and piano, appears here in two takes. The flip side, **People Are Meddling (In Our Affairs)**, was a personal declaration of independence: "I am my own boss, and I know what I want to do." Further sessions a year later produced a boogie-ing celebration of wedded bliss, **I Have Married**, and the steady-rolling **I'll Die Trying**.

J.B.'s apparent reluctance to take a guitar solo made it a wise move to add saxophonist J.T. Brown to the line-up for his next outing. He added fine contributions to the New Orleans-set **The Mojo** – an ancestor of Muddy Waters' signature piece – and two contrasting tunes, the moody **Slow Down Woman** and the upbeat **I Want My Baby**. All three feature here in two versions.

As well as more Lenoir gems – like **Play A Little While**, on which he finally essays a "Little Queenie"-style solo, the catchy instrumental **Bassology**, and his tribute to his wife, **Louise** – the CD is rounded off by a handful of tracks credited to Sunnyland Slim and Johnny Shines, on which J.B. supplied the rhythm guitar. Shines' Delta stylings make quite a contrast to Lenoir's brand of "Louisiana boogie", while his **Livin' In The White House** is a different kettle of fish to J.B.'s own acerbic "Eisenhower Blues", recorded for Parrot in 1954.

⮕ We almost chose **The Parrot Sessions**, Relic, 1989

53

J.B. Lenoir

Vietnam Blues

Evidence, 1995; recorded 1965–66

The two remarkable acoustic albums that J.B. Lenoir recorded shortly before his death in the mid-1960s, *Alabama Blues* and *Down In Mississippi* – now released on a single CD as **Vietnam Blues** – stand virtually alone in the canon of classic blues. Lenoir was always exceptional among Chicago bluesmen in tackling explicit social and political themes, but his decision to dispense with electric trappings and recast himself as a folk-style troubadour – in effect, a "protest singer" – was unique. While others among his peers made solo acoustic recordings, Lenoir did so as a vehicle for hard-hitting new songs about contemporary issues, rather than for nostalgic or commercial reasons.

These recordings are not simply obscure because Lenoir didn't live to capitalize on his achievement. In the early 1960s, J.B. had fallen on hard times. After leaving Chess in 1958, he recorded intermittently for several labels, and worked on developing what he called his "African Hunch" sound, which consisted of his own interpretation of African rhythms on both guitar and percussion. To support himself, he worked in the kitchens of the University of Illinois in Champaign. The material on *Vietnam Blues* originated on demo tapes Lenoir prepared with his former Chess cohort Willie Dixon and then circulated while touring the European festival circuit. They were eventually picked up by German promoter Horst Lippmann, who later recalled that "at the time no one was willing to release [them] in America because of the political content."

Willie Dixon supervised the recording of both *Alabama Blues* and *Down In Mississippi*. For Lippmann, present during the first sessions only, the brevity of the finished songs came as a shock. Several came in at under two minutes: "I almost fainted . . . Willie was thinking of making singles to fit onto the jukeboxes in America and I was thinking of making albums because nobody buys blues singles in Europe." While certain songs could certainly benefit from longer treatments, Lenoir and Dixon created two magnificent albums, which together have an overwhelming intensity.

Dixon didn't play bass at all. The only musicians were Lenoir on guitar – a far more sophisticated proposition than during his electric years – and veteran Chicago drummer Fred Below. Together they traded their patented "African Hunch" rhythms with superb invention, never more so than on I Feel So Good and Feelin' Good. In fact, most of *Vietnam Blues* has very little do with feeling good. Lenoir repeatedly addresses the ongoing Civil Rights struggle in utterly uncompromising terms. Thus Shot On James Meredith runs "June 6, 1966, they shot James Meredith down just like a dog/Mr President I wonder what are you going to do now/I don't believe you're gonna do nothing at all", while Down In Mississippi commemorates the land of Lenoir's birth with no sentimentality whatsoever: "I feel like I'm a lucky man, to get away with my life." Born Dead reaches an extraordinary peak of bitterness: "every black child born in Mississippi, you know the poor child is born dead."

Elsewhere, Lenoir delivers most of his best-known songs – like Talk To Your Daughter, Mojo Boogie, and Tax Payin' Blues, which was itself a remake of "Eisenhower Blues" – in appealingly stripped-down style, boogie-ing every bit as satisfyingly despite the lack of amplification. Round And Round is a newer dance number with a hypnotic rhythm, and Good Advice pays loving tribute to his grandmother's words of wisdom. Vietnam Blues itself was his final, powerful appeal to the powers that be: "Mr President you always cry about peace, but you must clean up your house before you leave."

➲ We almost chose **Fine Blues**, Official, 1990

Lightnin' Slim

Rooster Blues

El Diablo, 1998; recorded 1955–60

Those who like to see history in terms of inevitable progress would have a hard time explaining Lightnin' Slim. Perhaps the blues as a whole did develop from "primitive" prewar acoustic styles to the "sophisticated" postwar electric sound, but if so, down in the bayous of southwest Louisiana during the early 1950s, Slim took a very wrong turning indeed. The entire genre has few cruder specimens to offer than his early outings for Excello Records, in which he invented "swamp blues". Despite their stunning lack of originality and ludicrous technical deficiencies, however, they're enormously enjoyable to listen to. Above all, they have such a gloriously home-made feel, with Slim's sly, dirty voice riding atop a soupy mix composed largely of random percussive thumps on whatever happened to be lying around the studio.

Otis Hicks was around 30 when he learned to play guitar during the early 1940s, having moved to Louisiana from his native St Louis in his teens. Only able to play in the key of E natural, he modelled himself on Lightnin' Hopkins – hence the name, and the references to himself as "poor Lightnin'" – and began his career in the clubs of Baton Rouge. In 1954, a local DJ took him to meet Crowley-based entrepreneur J.D. Miller, for whose Feature and Excello labels he was to record for the next twelve years.

Rooster Blues collects eighteen of the finest products of those sessions. With endearing cheek, Slim is credited with writing them all, but most have very obvious antecedents in the work of Muddy Waters, John Lee Hooker and Jimmy Reed, to name but a few. Musically, Reed is the primary influence, with his gentle but insistent droning boogie and buzzing harp, while there's something of Chuck Berry in the insouciance of Slim's singing style. A strong personal charisma shines through, although for the brash boasting of so many Chicago bluesmen he tended to substitute abject self-pity, with song titles like Feelin' Awful Blues ("I woke up early this mornin', I was feelin' awful blue") and I Can't Be Successful.

It took a while for Slim to get the formula right. One early attempt, Goin' Home, is so heart-lurchingly slow (and out of tune) that it's easy to imagine that whoever's drumming is simply slapping Slim about the head with a rolled-up newspaper. Just Made Twenty One gets a nice rudimentary boogie going, but it's so clearly a copy of John Lee Hooker that it falls apart when Slim has to restrain himself from singing "Boogie Chillen".

In time, however, Slim came up with a stream of wry, quirky songs, and even a hit, in the shape of Rooster Blues, from 1959. Of the rest, It's Mighty Crazy is a masturbation epic dressed up as a ditty about doing the laundry, which boasts a guitar solo with almost no notes, and G.I. Slim is a humorous reworking of the "I'm A Man" motif in which he libellously asserts "I've shot dope with the King." Only one track here lasts longer than three minutes, and that by just five seconds; well over half are interrupted two-thirds of the way through by the drawled admonition, "well, blow your harmonica, son." Slim Harpo did the honours at first, then Lazy Lester took over even more effectively.

Lightnin' Slim's career with Excello came to an abrupt end in 1966, after he crashed Miller's truck and hightailed it to Detroit. He made a couple more albums before his death in 1974, but he never recaptured the splendid anarchy of his earlier days.

⮑ We almost chose **Nothing But The Devil**, Ace, 1996

55

Little Axe

The Wolf That House Built

Wired 27, 1995

The self-styled "ambient dub blues" of Little Axe was guaranteed to divide critics from the start. Even more than R.L. Burnside's *Come On In*, their 1994 debut album **The Wolf That House Built** simply uses the blues as its departure point, for a journey that carries it through the cavernous, echoing spaces that lie between soul, funk, reggae and trance. Its stated aim was to take the dub techniques usually used to deconstruct reggae, and set them to work on the blues instead. In the end, if that idea appeals to you, you'll probably love the album; if you're the kind to get hung up on whether it's really blues or not, you almost certainly won't.

Little Axe started life as the pet project of Ohio guitarist Skip McDonald, though he was joined by his two longtime cohorts, drummer Keith LeBlanc and bassist Doug Wimbish. Together they came to fame in late 1970s New York as the in-house rhythm section for pioneer rap label Sugarhill Records, playing on seminal singles like Grand Master Flash's "The Message" and Melle Mel's "White Lines". In the 1980s, they served the same function, with a higher profile, for On-U Sound in London. Working under such names as Tackhead and African Headcharge, they provided the multitextured but predominantly reggae-based beats on which producer Adrian Sherwood wrought his dub magic.

Skip McDonald's own roots lay in his father's love of blues, however, and *The Wolf That House Built* provided his chance to explore that tradition. The presence of a fourth band member, tabla player Talvin Singh – subsequently a winner of Britain's prestigious Mercury Music Prize – gave Little Axe an intriguing balance. For all its postmodern concept, the album keeps its feet on the ground through being as much acoustic as it is hi-tech, with both Singh and LeBlanc providing its percussive core on "real" not sequenced instruments.

With opening track Ride On (Fight On), McDonald skilfully sets out his stall, interweaving his own guitar with vocals sampled from Leadbelly, who also shares the writing credit. The "Wolf" of the album title is of course Howlin' Wolf, who makes a fleeting appearance with a sampled howl. He's back later on Wolf's Story, this time centre stage, recalling the origin of his nickname in a taped interview. LeBlanc's crisp, considered drumming beautifully highlights the rhythms of Wolf's voice, just as he'd done for Malcolm X on his own superb 1983 single, "Malcolm X".

Given the idea, the surprise of *The Wolf That House Built* is just how little sampling there actually is. Apart from a snatch of Son House's "Preaching Blues" at the start of Back To The Crossroads, it's up to Skip to provide the blues element in Adrian Sherwood's glorious, unpredictable mix. Whether in the searing lead of Never Turn Back, riding atop Singh's ferocious tablas, or the gentle strumming of Another Sinful Day, he does a magnificent job.

Once you've got over the "dub" side of things, there's another problematic word in the Little Axe mission statement: "ambient". The charge has been levelled that this is just superior background music, and it has to be said that most of *The Wolf*'s eleven tracks are not really songs at all, let alone twelve-bar blues. Some consist of swirling, amorphous soundscapes that simply wash over you; others, like Wake The Town, which lifts its vocal line from U-Roy's 1970 reggae hit, might just as easily turn up on a Tackhead album. If you must have twelve-bar blues, there are 99 other CDs filled with blues songs in this book; for a taste of what the blues can be, or perhaps even will be, buy this one.

➲ We almost chose **Slow Fuse**, Wired, 1999

56

Little Milton

The Complete Stax Singles

Stax, 1994; recorded 1971–75

"Little Milton" Campbell is one of those bluesmen who seems to have been around forever. He left his family home in Inverness, Mississippi, before he was 20, and he's been on the road for nearly fifty years. As singer, guitarist and songwriter, he's always moved with the times, however, and even if he hasn't achieved a great deal of recognition beyond his black Southern constituency, he's always been dependable for his own quality brand of soul/blues fusion. In live appearances these days, he often shares the billing with Bobby Bland; while not quite in the same league, he's carved out a similar persona, as a wry, rich-voiced chronicler of marital infidelities and midlife regrets.

Like so many aspiring blues performers in the early 1950s, the young Milton Campbell idolized T-Bone Walker, and was encouraged in his own ambitions by the advent of B.B. King – his earliest recordings, made with the "Playmates of Rhythm" for Memphis's Sun label in 1953, were very much in the B.B. King mould. After working with Meteor and Bobbin later that decade, he spent the 1960s with Chess subsidiary Checker. There he enjoyed sixteen R&B chart hits, climaxing with 1969's "Grits Ain't Groceries".

Checker encouraged Little Milton in melding blues with soul – specifically, in cutting brassy, punchy mid-tempo versions of what were at heart slow blues ballads – but his personal synthesis reached its purest expression when he moved back to Memphis to work with Stax Records in 1971. Nobody handled brass better than Stax, as Albert King's work had amply demonstrated (see p.91), and the potential for interplay between Stax's horn and rhythm sections and a strong blues guitarist was tailor-made for Little Milton. **The Complete Stax Singles** – the A- and B-sides of his ten releases over the next four years – shows how well he rose to the challenge.

He certainly hit the ground running. Debut If That Ain't A Reason is a gloriously funky saga of advice to married men – "your wife's name is Betty, you keep calling her Jean" – that simply radiates Milton's zest for the job, and even throws in a harmonica solo for good measure. Follow-up That's What Love Will Make You Do has an equally infectious bass-driven beat, this time with Milton's fluid guitar jabbering away at double time all over everything.

The classic for which Milton's Stax years are best remembered, however, is his third release. Walking The Back Streets And Crying – a Sandy Jones ballad also covered by Albert King – appears here in a sumptuous six-minute version, building inexorably in both the depth of emotion in his singing and the searing intensity of his guitar solo. There's equally powerful guitar work to be found on the swaggering Who Can Handle Me Is You and the relentless, driving Tin Pan Alley. On If You Talk In Your Sleep, from 1974, it's Milton's singing that captivates. Elvis had recorded the song at Stax the previous year, and Milton makes good on his boast that "we probably won't sell the kind of records that he sells but we can damn sure do this song better than he did it." The one false note is the remake of Behind Closed Doors, which starts out well enough but turns horrible as the chorus arrives.

Stax was falling apart by 1975, when Milton recorded the final track here, Packed Up And Took My Mind. Part-written by Denise LaSalle, it presaged his next major career move. After a few lean years, he found a new spiritual home alongside Bobby Bland at Malaco Records, where he's still going strong a dozen albums later.

➲ We almost chose **Greatest Hits**, Chess, 1997

57

Little Walter

His Best – The Chess 50th Anniversary Collection

MCA/Chess, 1997; recorded 1952–60

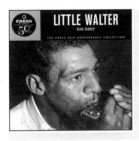

Most things about the blues are open to argument, but when it comes to harmonica players there's no disputing who was the greatest of them all – Little Walter. And since Chess have finally replaced their two separate volumes of *The Best Of Little Walter* with this twenty-track compilation, **His Best**, there is no question as to the most essential CD release. A chronological run-through of his finest work from 1952 up to 1960 – a period in which he boasted fifteen R&B chart hits (a total only exceeded by Muddy Waters) – it's a fabulous monument to Walter's artistry, invention and sheer variety.

Marion Walter Jacobs' life was more of a horror story than a fairy tale, and it didn't have a happy ending. Born in Marksville, Louisiana, in 1930, he was on the road by the age of 8. and had his own radio show at 15. By the time he joined Muddy Waters' band in Chicago in 1948, he'd received personal tuition on the harp from both Sonny Boy Williamsons and "Big Walter" Horton, but had also drawn inspiration from the saxophone style of Louis Jordan.

Little Walter's four-year stint in the Muddy Waters band's first – and arguably best – incarnation came to an abrupt end in 1952. An instrumental they'd been using as a live theme song, "Your Cat Will Play", was released by Chess as Juke, and credited to Little Walter and his Night Cats. As soon as it hit, Walter walked out on a Louisiana tour and raced back to Chicago, where he linked up with the Four Aces – the previous fourth

Ace, harp player Junior Wells, moved over to Muddy in turn and embarked on a solo career. Walter nonetheless continued to play on Muddy's records until 1956 and indeed lived in his basement on and off until he died.

For Muddy, the split had been inevitable: Walter "was *wild*, he had to play *fast*." While "Juke" was bursting with energy, however, it was also more channelled and disciplined than that description might suggest. Walter's harp sounds at first more like a sax, playing structured jazz-like improvisations around the central theme. Previously the harp had been a subsidiary instrument, blown close to a stand-up microphone; Walter's great innovation was to hold both harp and a mike with its own amp in his hands, and play the two together. This gave the potential not only for volume but also for a wide range of amplified, distorted effects. With the Aces, Walter was free to play lead, backed by two guitarists (the Myers brothers) but no bassist, and underpinned by the deft jazz-tinged drumming of Fred Below.

Showpiece Aces instrumentals ranged from the mournful Sad Hours to the urgent Off The Wall, but Walter's success owed much to his other, less celebrated talent: his poised, knowing vocal style. My Babe, Willie Dixon's reworking of the gospel standard "This Train", and the menacing Boom, Boom Out Goes The Light, were his most characterful performances, but on less formal songs such as Blues With A Feeling and Mellow Down Easy, which were basically vehicles for extended harmonica workouts, his singing beautifully complements his virtuosity.

Walter's last hit came in 1959, with the sadly unprophetic Everything's Gonna Be Alright. Only the final track here, 1960's Just Your Fool, was recorded after his 30th birthday, but by then he was old before his time. The European blues revival came too late to compensate for the loss of his star status at home, or to rescue him from increasingly bitter, belligerent alcoholism. He died in Chicago in 1968, following a run-of-the-mill street brawl.

➲ We almost chose **The Essential Little Walter**, MCA, 1993

58

Magic Sam

West Side Soul

Delmark, 1990; recorded 1967

Because of his sudden death from a heart attack in December 1969, at the age of just 32, guitarist Magic Sam tends to be remembered as one of the might-have-beens – yet another doomed figure in the tragic blues tradition. While his life may have been cut short, however, his promise was far from unfulfilled. Two years earlier, he'd made what remains the greatest Chicago blues album of all time. Of course, Muddy Waters, Howlin' Wolf and many others left a legacy of stunning individual singles, but in **West Side Soul** Magic Sam produced the most coherent, sustained testament of urban blues imaginable.

West Side Soul was recorded at the tail end of Chicago's pre-eminence in the blues, and indeed at a time when the blues itself seemed poised to enter a terminal decline. Although barely 30, however, Samuel Maghett was a veteran of the scene. Born in Mississippi in 1937, he moved to Chicago with his family at the age of 13, and worked his way up through the clubs of the West Side in competition and conjunction with his similarly transplanted contemporaries Buddy Guy and Otis Rush. He took the name "Magic Sam", a play on his surname, when he first recorded for the Cobra label in 1957, spurning Cobra's own suggestion of "Sad Sam". For the next ten years, he moved from label to label, and also spent a brief unhappy period in the army.

By the time he arrived at Delmark in 1967, he was ready to break through. Despite countless easily recognizable components and influences, *West Side Soul* is very clearly his record. It's his name on the sleeve, and the band stays in the background throughout. He chose not to use his regular harp player, while the piano stool, in the absence of his preferred accompanist Otis Spann, was occupied by a Swedish tourist (credited as "Stockholm Slim"), who's inaudible on all but one track.

Delmark boss Bob Koester reportedly signed Sam for his singing rather than his guitar playing. In truth, he stands head and shoulders above his Chicago rivals, not so much because he wrings every nuance from the words, but because his voice functions as an instrument in such perfect accord with his guitar. Both operate for the most part in the higher ranges, forever inching towards the brink of all-out frenzy yet still retaining a perfect clarity and fluency.

While there's great variety on this album, the overall vision remains consistent. On the opening track, That's All I Need – the album's closest approach to the then-current pop-soul sound – and on the relatively slow All Of Your Love, Sam's voice tends to overshadow the rest of the mix, while the John Lee Hooker-style instrumental Lookin' Good is a virtuoso guitar boogie.

Other high points include the moment when Sam's guitar is first unleashed, for an extended five-minute workout on I Need You So Bad; the frenetic, exuberant boogie of Junior Parker's I Feel So Good; and a classic rendition of Sweet Home Chicago that's the very essence of Chicago blues. Magic Sam was on the point of signing to Stax when he died, a move you can't help feeling might have diluted his hard-edged, knife-through-butter blues power. On the other hand, it's striking to realize the degree to which his vocal mannerisms were derived from soul stylists such as Sam Cooke (especially on his live recordings) and Otis Redding. I Don't Want No Woman, for example, was first cut by Bobby Bland in the 1950s, but the two alternative takes that appear here are far more overtly "soulful" than Bland's original.

⮑ We almost chose **Black Magic**, Delmark, 1994

59

Percy Mayfield

Poet Of The Blues

Specialty, 1990; recorded 1950–54

While Percy Mayfield is often hailed as the greatest songwriter the blues has produced, calling him a "poet" might lead you to expect lyrics bursting with hellhounds, devils, and blues like showers of rain. In fact, he wrote simple songs about ordinary human emotions; that they communicated so effectively with his audience was due as much to his genius as a singer as to his words. **Poet Of The Blues** collects 25 of those songs, cut during his brief heyday at the start of the 1950s. Imbued with mystery and melancholy, they were enormously popular and, although Mayfield's smooth baritone hardly fits modern conceptions of the blues, they remain hauntingly atmospheric and powerful.

Born in Louisiana in 1920, Mayfield made his home in California during World War II. Modelling himself on Nat "King" Cole, he ranked alongside Charles Brown as the most prominent of the "sepia Sinatras" who dominated the state's postwar blues scene. His debt to jazz and swing was always obvious, both in his intimate delivery and his big-band accompaniments. Mayfield's first break came in 1947, when he stepped into the breach after Jimmy Witherspoon failed to turn up at a Supreme Records session to record the Mayfield-penned "Two Years Of Torture".

Poet Of The Blues picks up the story in 1950, with Mayfield's first recording for Art Rupe's Specialty label. Please Send Me Someone To Love adroitly blended a general prayer for world peace with his own personal sorrow: "just because I'm in misery, I don't beg for sympathy, but if it's not asking too much, please send me someone to love." An extra air of introspection came from his trick of repeating the last few words of a line as though to himself, before continuing with the next. Striking a chord with a nation immersed in the Korean War, it was an immediate #1 hit and established Mayfield's image as a suave crooner, sharply dressed in a smart suit as he imparted a slow blues ballad.

Over the next two years, Mayfield enjoyed six more chart entries, following much the same formula. Bandleader Maxwell Davis always had at least three saxes on hand to back Mayfield up, and threw in a tenor sax solo of his own, and there'd usually be a gentle, looping guitar solo from Gene Phillips into the bargain. Two of the finest tracks featured strong piano interludes – Strange Things Happening (which pleaded "If you know you don't love me, Why won't you let me be") and Lost Love.

Right from the start, there was an overriding theme of loss and pain: witness titles such as Prayin' For Your Return, Hopeless and Life Is Suicide. Perhaps the best remembered is the doom-laden The River's Invitation, as covered by Aretha Franklin. Whether or not those were premonitions, disaster soon struck. A car crash in 1952 damaged Mayfield's looks and self-confidence so severely that he withdrew from live performing for over a decade.

Though his chart days seemed over, Mayfield continued to record, sounding more haunted than ever. On Memory Pain – later reworked by John Lee Hooker as "It Serves Me Right To Suffer"– he seemed filled with self-reproach: "I don't see well, I'm absent minded, I hardly sleep at all, My past has put me on a habit of nicotine and alcohol, It serves me right to suffer."

Mayfield eventually returned to prominence with Ray Charles, for whom he wrote "Hit The Road Jack" and three other Top 10 hits. He was also responsible for Elvis's "Stranger In My Home Town", and was recording and performing up to his death in 1984.

➲ We almost chose **Memory Pain**, Specialty, 1992

60

Jimmy McCracklin

The Walk: Jimmy McCracklin At His Best

Razor & Tie, 1997; recorded 1956–69

Despite California's high profile in the music industry, blues purists often dismiss the West Coast blues scene as peripheral. By such reckoning, the true flame of the blues was carried from the rural Deep South up to the urban industrial North, while black musicians living beside the Pacific lost touch with the wellspring and became too ready to water down their heritage with the latest mainstream fad. Certainly, while "the blues" remains so closely identified with the music made by Delta migrants in postwar Chicago and Detroit, it is much harder to categorize the sounds produced by their black contemporaries out on the West Coast. Jimmy McCracklin ranks high among the many LA-based performers whose achievements have been neglected as a result. As the twenty tracks collected on **The Walk** anthology amply testify, McCracklin's talents – as vocalist, pianist and, especially, songwriter – were richly varied, but the fact that they ranged beyond the blues should not deny him the recognition he deserves.

Although he insists on a birth date of August 1931, the fact that Jimmy McCracklin served in the navy in California during World War II suggests him to be a good ten years older. After the war, rather than return to his hometown of St Louis, McCracklin stayed out West. An automobile accident cut short his career as a light heavyweight boxer, so he started to trade on his Walter Davis-style piano skills. McCracklin was in some way involved with Roy Hawkins' original recording of "The Thrill Is Gone" in Oakland in 1951. His claims to have written the B.B.

King chestnut have never been accepted, but he was clearly developing as a songwriter, with a knack for combining punchy lyrics with catchy piano or sax hooks.

By the time McCracklin cut Get Back for Premium Records, in 1956, he'd worked with a dozen different labels. Credited to Jimmy McCracklin And His Orchestra, it showcased his assured singing over a big-band accompaniment, plus a heavy rhythmic nod towards rock'n'roll. His next release took things a stage further; cut on a self-produced session at a cost of $11, The Walk was a shameless but irresistible novelty record, designed so he said to prove how simple it was to meet the tastes of the rock'n'roll audience. Propelled by a deep echoey bass riff, adorned with name checks for Suzie Q and various dance crazes, and topped by hand-claps and sax solos, it was a national pop hit on Checker in 1958.

That success led to McCracklin's signing for Mercury, and a succession of similarly enjoyable follow-ups, including The Georgia Slop and The Wobble, both included here, and "Let's Do It (The Chicken Scratch)", which unfortunately is not. Perhaps because they seemed aimed at adult blacks (rather than teenage whites), none sold especially well.

The disappointed McCracklin then set up his own label, Art-Tone, and returned to a more overtly blues-based sound. Throughout the early 1960s, he released a steady stream of self-penned ballads, delivered in a stentorian gospel-tinged voice reminiscent of Solomon Burke. Just Got To Know, (Take) Advice and The Bitter And The Sweet were all magnificent, but the peak came in 1965, when he hooked up with Bobby Bland's horn section at Don Robey's studios in Houston to create Think. Even if McCracklin has spoken of its "beautiful message", it's as cynical an anti-love song as it's possible to imagine: "I could give up my woman, You could give up your man, But it don't make sense to take the chance." The horns do their utmost, and there's a great sax solo, but McCracklin himself, on both piano and vocals, is the commanding presence, delivering a performance to match any of the acknowledged blues greats.

➲ We almost chose **The Mercury Recordings**, Bear Family, 1994

Mississippi Fred McDowell

The First Recordings

Rounder, 1997; recorded 1959

Every now and then, the fantasy of the authentic, backwoods bluesman playing his music purely for pleasure turns out to be true; rarely so spectacularly as in the case of singer-guitarist Mississippi Fred McDowell. In stumbling across McDowell during a field trip through the Mississippi hill country in 1959, folklorist Alan Lomax encountered not only a genuine original, but a master of a relatively unknown sub-genre of the blues.

Lomax had been the first to record Muddy Waters in the Delta in 1941, while his father John "discovered" the songster Leadbelly in a Louisiana prison in 1934. McDowell was something else again. Only a handful of the fourteen tracks now included on Rounder's **The First Recordings**, captured on Lomax's portable reel-to-reel tape recorder during their first meeting, were actually released at the time. Those were enough, however, to reveal McDowell as mining an older and more recognizably African vein of the blues than either Waters or Leadbelly. In many respects, his music bears a closer resemblance to the equally little-known tradition anthologized on *The Real Bahamas* (see p.197) than it does to the Delta blues produced thirty miles west of his home.

Mississippi Fred McDowell was actually born in Tennessee, not far east of Memphis, in 1904. Though old enough to have seen Charlie Patton perform live, he himself had never been recorded until September 1959, when Alan Lomax came to his farm outside Como.

McDowell's playing technique consisted of two quite distinct strands. The first was his piercing slide work on the treble strings – his original "bottleneck" was a hollowed-out piece of cattle-bone – while the second was his strongly plucked single-note runs on the bass. While the one doesn't preclude the other, his songs tend to fall into two categories, depending on which aspect was to the fore on each. When his emphasis was on the slide, he sounded reminiscent of Blind Willie Johnson. Not only did he play Johnson standards like Keep Your Lamps Trimmed And Burning, but (like Johnson) he would also "voice" specific words on his guitar rather than play them, as on Wished I Was In Heaven Sitting Down.

When McDowell chose to stress the bass instead, he churned out a steady droning boogie that seemed all his own. The local community knew him as "Shake 'Em" on account of his trademark piece in that style, Shake 'Em On Down, which had previously been recorded by Bukka White. On his fabulously idiosyncratic reinterpretation of the song here, he's joined by neighbour Miles Pratcher on second guitar, while his sister Fanny Davis buzzes dementedly on a comb wrapped in toilet paper. That home-made approximation of the hill country's "fife and drum" bands is echoed on What's The Matter Now?, where a sweeping broom provides minimal percussion behind the endlessly repeating rhythm.

When Lomax played these recordings back to McDowell, "he stomped up and down on the porch, whooping and laughing . . . He knew he had been heard and felt his fortune had been made." In fact, it was another five years before Chris Strachwitz of Arhoolie Records rolled up to record him again, but the second time around McDowell did indeed establish a reputation that kept him going for the rest of the 1960s, through several albums and countless live appearances. Before he died in 1972, he even had a taste of the big time, when the Rolling Stones covered his version of "You Gotta Move" on their *Sticky Fingers* album.

⮑ We almost chose **Shake 'Em On Down**, Rhino, 1998

Blind Willie McTell

Complete Recorded Works Vol.1

Document, 1994; recorded 1927–31

Blind Willie McTell occupies a unique place in blues history. Not only did he combine a consummate mastery of the twelve-string guitar with a delicate and expressive vocal style, but he also sustained a recording career through four decades, while remaining at heart an old-style itinerant bluesman. A conspicuous presence on the streets of Atlanta until his death in 1959, he was the last of the great songsters. So thoroughly did he personalize his repertoire that it's impossible to assess how much he actually wrote, but his best performances are autobiographical masterpieces of the highest order.

For all its length, Blind Willie McTell's career was never more compelling than at its outset. Despite its dull packaging and somewhat sketchy sleeve notes, Document's first volume of the **Complete Recorded Works** is the obvious place to start.

Willie McTell's real name remains a mystery, but he was born in 1898 in Thomson, Georgia. His family name was McTear or McTier, while his Christian name may have been Willie, Samuel or even Eddie (his tombstone reads "Eddie McTier"). Neither is it clear whether he was always blind or lost his sight completely when he was in his twenties. Raised in Statesboro, not far from Savannah, he spent a few years in a touring medicine show. Spells at blind schools in Macon and New York taught him to read text and music in Braille. Somewhere on the road, he teamed up with Blind Willie Johnson, which may explain the earliest of his many pseudonyms – Blind Willie McTell.

For his first session, in Atlanta in October 1927 – on which he played six-string guitar – McTell's brief from Victor Records was to perform country blues in the vein of Blind Lemon Jefferson. He obliged with two creditable genre pieces, Writin' Paper Blues and Stole Rider Blues, and one genuine classic, Mama 'Tain't Long 'Fo' Day, in which his youthful, almost feminine voice chimes beautifully with the plaintive lyrics and slide guitar.

Victor signed McTell to a four-year contract, and he returned to Atlanta the next October to record a further four sides, including the magnificent Statesboro Blues. Picked fast but with crystal-clear precision, it's a poignant and much-covered tour de force "Mother died and left me reckless, daddy died and left me wild/I'm not good lookin' but I'm some sweet woman's angel child."

Next time McTell stepped into the studio, in October 1929, it was for Columbia, for whom he moved away from pure blues towards less structured pieces from his vaudeville days. Both Atlanta Strut and Travelin' Blues are medleys of catchphrases and random verses strung together with a talking-blues narration; they abound in instrumental stunt work, whether it be astonishingly dexterous finger-picking, deft changes of rhythm, or impersonations ranging through voices, pianos, bells, cornets, whistles and even chickens. If you need convincing that, as Bob Dylan declared "nobody sings the blues like Blind Willie McTell", listen to the surreal intensity with which he orders his eggs "scrambled down"; this is a man who could sing the phone book and still make you cry your eyes out. As much because his previous records had failed to sell as to conceal his identity from Victor, these sides were released as being by "Blind Sammie".

Following some relatively undistinguished Victor cuts from 1929, the CD concludes with six superb sides McTell recorded in 1930 and 1931, as both Blind Sammie for Columbia and Georgia Bill for OKeh. Razor Ball, Southern Can Is Mine and Broke Down Engine Blues remained in his repertoire for the rest of his life, but his fingers were never quite as nimble again, nor his voice so achingly pure.

➲ We almost chose **The Early Years 1927–33**, Yazoo, 1991

Blind Willie McTell

Atlanta Twelve String

Atlantic, 1992; recorded 1949

For a man who never had a hit, Blind Willie McTell made an awful lot of records and his musical progress is more thoroughly documented than any of the other early country blues greats. Perhaps the most unlikely session of McTell's entire career was cut for Atlantic Records in 1949. Atlantic had existed for a mere two years, primarily as a jazz label, when owner Ahmet Ertegun, hearing that McTell was still active in Atlanta, rushed down to record him. Such enthusiasm makes it all the stranger that only two of his fifteen sides were released, under the name of "Barrelhouse Sammy (The Country Boy)". For blues collectors, the search for further fruits of this mysterious session was something akin to the grail quest, and was rewarded in 1969 when the tapes were discovered misplaced in Atlantic's vaults.

Issued as **Atlanta Twelve String** in 1972, the results were better than anyone had dared to hope. Just to hear a master of prewar rural blues recorded on high-fidelity modern equipment is a real treat – the deep, resonant sound of his twelve-string guitar is absolutely gorgeous – but McTell was also on top form. His skills had been honed by thirty years as a professional entertainer, mostly performing for tips at Atlanta restaurants such as the white-only Pig'n'Whistle chain of barbecue stands (hence yet another nickname, Pig'n'Whistle Red), but also playing for tourists in Florida and the Sea Islands. With maturity, he'd also acquired a certain world-weariness. He now sang in a much deeper register, touched with a slight croak or rasp and, even though his material was little changed, he seemed far more concerned with death and loss than with the plaintive love songs of his youth. That contrast, between the earnest, lightning-fast virtuoso of the 1920s and the grizzled veteran of 1949, is what makes *Atlanta Twelve String* such a moving and satisfying album.

The two tracks that had already seen the light of day were the brisk rag Kill It Kid, and McTell's fourth rendition of Broke Down Engine Blues, taken more slowly and with greater precision than his 1930s versions. Another remake, The Razor Ball, bore almost no lyrical similarity to earlier performances. Throughout the session, McTell can be heard exhorting himself to "kick it, six", or to "play that thing low and lonesome, boy"; some critics have suggested that longtime associate Curley Weaver may have been present, but it's more likely he played all the parts himself. His instrumental prowess is best displayed on two standout tracks, Pinetop's Boogie Woogie and Motherless Children Have A Hard Time. The former, a much-loved piano standard first recorded by Clarence "Pinetop" Smith in 1928, features some startling piano-like percussive effects. The latter is modelled closely on Blind Willie Johnson's 1927 version, but uses a twelve-string (as opposed to Johnson's six-string), thus facilitating some stimulating interplay between the bass runs, treble fills and the singing.

Despite the inclusion of four overt gospel songs, and his subsequent stint as a preacher, McTell was happy to perform earthy, vernacular material, and the real bravura triumph here is the astonishing Dying Crapshooter's Blues. He'd recorded the piece in 1940, and claimed to have written it, although it's clearly based on the traditional "Streets Of Laredo". In a cavalcade of flamboyant imagery, quite the match of anything Dylan ever managed, it chronicles the demise of Jesse the "wild reckless gambler", whose "heart was hard and cold as ice" and who, after being gunned down by the police, instructs his mourners to "dig my grave with the ace of spades" and "let a deck of cards be my tombstone."

➲ We almost chose **Pig'n'Whistle Red**, Biograph, 1993

Memphis Minnie

Bumble Bee

Indigo, 1995; recorded 1929–41

When it comes to Memphis Minnie, the usual blues stereotypes barely apply. First and most obviously, she was a woman. She wasn't the only female blues artist in the 1920s and 1930s, of course, but none of the others was so accomplished as both instrumentalist and singer, or kept going so long into the electric, postwar era. Neither was Minnie poor or obscure: she was a true star, and acted the part, feeling duty-bound to display fine cars and expensive clothes to her adoring public. She's often considered an exponent of rural rather than urban blues, but that surely stems from canny catering to popular tastes rather than her intrinsic nature. As the wide-ranging **Bumble Bee** compilation demonstrates, her style changed repeatedly, with no one period any more "authentic" than the rest.

Memphis Minnie was really New Orleans Lizzie. She was born Elizabeth Douglas in Algiers, Louisiana, in 1897, directly across the Mississippi from the French Quarter of New Orleans. By 1910, however, she had moved to Memphis. Barring a spell touring with the Ringling Brothers Circus, she spent the next twenty years there learning her craft, playing guitar and banjo on Beale Street. "Kid Douglas", as she was known, also teamed up with the first of the three guitarists she was to marry: Casey Bill Weldon of the Memphis Jug Band.

In 1929, a record company scout whisked Minnie and her second husband, Kansas Joe McCoy, off to New York. McCoy was the featured attraction first time around, with his powerful

When The Levee Breaks, one of many such chronicles of the great Mississippi Flood of 1927. Within months, however, the newly renamed Memphis Minnie had a huge hit in her own right. The exuberant sexual imagery of **Bumble Bee**, in which she sang of a "stinger as long as my right arm" and begged "sting me bumble bee until I get enough", won her national acclaim. In due course, the song transmuted into Muddy Waters' "Honey Bee".

As was standard practice, the duo quickly re-recorded their signature tune for several different labels, and in the process wound up living in Chicago. All the remaining tracks on this CD were cut there, and Minnie was to stay in the Windy City until 1957. Though much of her early-1930s material dealt with country themes – witness **Frankie Jean That Trottin' Fool**, the saga of her papa's pet hog – Minnie herself lived the high city life. She triumphed over both Big Bill Broonzy and Tampa Red in a famed guitar-playing contest, and her weekly "Blue Monday" parties became legendary.

It's impossible now to be sure who played which part in her duets with McCoy, but the deft fingering on instrumentals like **Let's Go To Town** and **Picking The Blues** is generally assumed to be Minnie's. Certainly, she kept up the standard after that marriage broke up. She worked with a pianist or small band as often as with a second guitarist, even after her third marriage, to Little Son Joe.

During the mid-1930s, such Minnie songs as **Where Is My Good Man At?** tended to explore conventional wronged-woman, cheating-man narratives, without any great sense that they held true for her personally. She revitalized her career in 1941, however, with the much more worldly, upbeat **Me And My Chauffeur Blues**. That was to carry her through another decade at the top of the Chicago tree, handling the electric guitar as nimbly as she had her old metal-bodied National. Ultimately, after stints with both Chess and JOB, she moved back to Memphis, where she died in 1973.

➲ We almost chose **Hoodoo Lady**, Columbia, 1991

65

Memphis Slim

At The Gate Of Horn

Charly, 1999; recorded 1958–59

An almost overwhelming proportion of Memphis Slim's output during his fifty-year recording career is available on CD, but there's no better place to start than with **At The Gate Of Horn**. Cut for Vee Jay Records on a single day in August 1959, and re-released with four bonus tracks from January 1958, it serves effectively as a compilation of his greatest hits played by his greatest band. The title is misleading in several ways. Not only was the set not recorded at the Chicago nightclub The Gate Of Horn, it's not even a live album at all. Furthermore, The Gate Of Horn specialized in what was then called folk and would now perhaps be termed world or acoustic music, and the use of its name here marks an early attempt to market blues to a folk audience. However, the album itself consists of urbane, sophisticated big-band blues rather than the downhome style to which Memphis Slim, like so many others, was to gravitate over the next few years.

Memphis Slim started out as the archetypal barrelhouse pianist. By the age of 16, in 1931, he was pumping out the boogie on Beale Street in his native Memphis, where he'd taken over the piano stool at the legendary Midway Café from his idol Roosevelt Sykes. His real name was Peter Chatman, which even then made him blues royalty – several of his uncles, who collectively formed the nucleus of the Mississippi Sheiks, achieved solo success, including Sam Chatman and Bo Chatman (as Bo Carter). Slim himself moved to Chicago at the end of the

1930s, when the major labels stopped coming to Memphis to record the blues, and swiftly became Big Bill Broonzy's resident pianist. He was soon cutting discs for Bluebird – his first session, in 1940, was "Diggin' My Potatoes" with Washboard Sam – OKeh, and countless other imprints.

By the time of *At The Gate Of Horn*, twenty years on, Memphis Slim had long been established in his own right. He'd previously released versions of several of the selections included here, and some had become hits for artists such as Joe Williams and Count Basie. In fact, he was already something of an elder statesman, leading his own highly accomplished band, and the album is as much a showcase for their skills as it is for his own instrumental prowess. If anything, his piano consistently plays second fiddle to the fluid, flamboyant guitar work of Matt Murphy, whose jazz-tinged solos adorn tracks like Lend Me Your Love and Messin' Around. Add three sublime saxophonists, plus Slim's cousin Sam Chatman (Junior) on bass, and you've got the perfect recipe for cool Chicago blues – they could even sing, as witnessed by the delicious ensemble effort on Stroll On Little Girl.

Within three years of these Vee Jay sessions, Slim had moved permanently to Paris, where he married a French woman and re-styled himself "The Ambassador of the Blues". Understandably, he preferred being fêted in Europe to being on the receiving end of racism back home: "I fought the shit a long time and then I got out of it." The measured dignity of his singing and the overt philosophizing of his songs no doubt held a particular appeal to French sensibilities. That side of his character receives full expression on *At The Gate Of Horn*, with introspective ballads such as Slim's Blues and Mother Earth proceeding at a stately tempo far removed from the dance-club pyrotechnics of his youth. There's also space, however, for sprightly workouts like Rockin' The House and Sassy Mae (a variation of "Dust My Broom"), so the album in its entirety delivers a satisfying, rounded portrait of one of the most powerful personalities in blues history.

➲ We almost chose **Lonely Nights**, Catfish, 1999

66

Big Maceo Merriweather

The Best Of Big Maceo

Arhoolie, 1992; recorded 1941–45

No musician so perfectly epitomizes the transition between the prewar and postwar, rural and urban, styles of blues as Big Maceo Merriweather. In adapting and updating the barrelhouse sound, he did for the piano what B.B. King and T-Bone Walker did for the guitar, and what Sonny Boy Williamson I and Little Walter did for the harmonica. Had his health lasted, he would probably have become the linchpin of the 1950s Chicago blues scene. As it is, a stroke in 1946 cost him the use of his right hand and, with almost unbearable poignancy, though he continued to pound out traditional bass rhythms with his left, on his final dates the "modern" treble flourishes had to be played by young protégés like Eddie Boyd and Otis Spann.

Despite the impression given by songs such as Texas Blues – "my home's in Texas, what am I doing up here?" – Maceo Merriweather came from Georgia. Having started out playing in Atlanta, he moved to Detroit at the age of 19 in 1924, and found work at Ford Motors. By the time his sister prompted him to audition for Lester Melrose's Bluebird label in Chicago, he was a firm favourite in the clubs of Hastings Street.

All but three of the 28 sides Maceo recorded during his heyday appear in chronological order on Arhoolie's **The Best Of Big Maceo: The King Of Chicago Blues Piano**. Veteran guitarist Tampa Red is present throughout. Used to working in tandem with pianists from "Georgia Tom" Dorsey onwards, he's a superbly sympathetic accompanist, but the talents of Big Maceo always occupy centre stage. Maceo was not a blistering boogie-woogie merchant: his trademark was rhythm rather than speed. The power and precision of his bass runs owed as much to his being left-handed as it did to his huge size. He was also blessed with a fine, lushly intimate singing voice, which radiated warmth even through the most mournful material.

Maceo's first session produced his biggest hit. **Worried Life Blues**, often informally known as "Lordy Lord", was his re-working of Sleepy John Estes' 1935 record "Someday Baby". Its doleful refrain of "someday baby, I ain't gonna worry my life any more", struck a chord nationally, and he returned repeatedly to the same tune and theme for the rest of his career. **County Jail**, an equally heartfelt tale of woe, saw Maceo bemoaning "these stripes don't hurt me, but these chains they kill me dead", while the more upbeat **Can't You Read** entertainingly interprets the popular folk tale about the monkey and the baboon.

Although his new-found reputation made Maceo a popular live attraction, and he toured successfully with Big Bill Broonzy among others, he fell on hard times when the American Federation of Musicians imposed a two-year ban on recording to combat the menace of the jukebox. When he returned to the studio in 1945, he announced that his worries were over in a new version of "Worried Life Blues", **Things Have Changed**. Reflecting the changes in popular taste, almost all the fruits of his final sessions were performed at much faster tempos than before. **Kidman Blues** was a brisk traditional number, while **Texas Stomp** was adorned with prototype Fats Domino triplets. Best of all was a rare instrumental, the flamboyant **Chicago Breakdown**. Sadly, it was Maceo's swansong; six months later without the use of his right hand (and with the experiment of using his left hand only proving short-lived) his career was effectively over. Despite cutting a few more sides as a vocalist, he was unable to make a comeback. He died in 1953.

➲ We almost chose **Victor/Bluebird Recordings 1945–47**, RCA, 1997

67

Mississippi Sheiks

Stop And Listen

Yazoo, 1992; recorded 1930–35

Though it's the names of lonesome, devil-driven bluesmen like Robert Johnson and Charlie Patton that have passed into legend, the most popular black musicians in prewar Mississippi saw themselves as entertainers pure and simple. The Mississippi Sheiks took their name in homage to silent movie actor Rudolph Valentino (star of *The Sheik*), and even if their records were pitched primarily within the "race" market they made their living playing to both black and white audiences. While most of the twenty tracks on the compilation **Stop And Listen** are recognizable as blues, the Sheiks mark the final flourish of the string-based rural dance tradition before black and white music, as blues and country, went their separate ways.

For live performances the Sheiks might field up to a dozen members, but on record they were basically a duo. Lonnie Chatmon, from Boston, Mississippi (known as "Big Guff"), played the fiddle, while his childhood neighbour Walter Vinson supported him on guitar and handled the singing. Vinson took up music because he "got tired of smellin' mule farts"; for Chatmon, it was in the blood. One of the eleven sons of Henderson Chatmon, he started out with five siblings as the Chatmon Brothers. It was the Chatmons who formed the core of the Sheiks as a live act; including Armenter Chatmon, better known as Bo Carter, there were enough for the Sheiks to field two separate line-ups when they were double-booked.

Vinson and Lonnie Chatmon were such close friends they called each other "Bruno" and everyone else "Doc". They first teamed up in the mid-1920s, but the turning point in their career came one morning in Itta Bena in 1930, when Vinson started fooling around with a song he called Sitting On Top Of The World. By the time he'd finished writing it, they'd earned $19 in tips. Perfect for a white dance called the One Step, and snapped up by OKeh Records producer Polk Brockman when they played it for him in Shreveport, Louisiana, the song swiftly sold over a million copies. Later covered by artists as disparate as Howlin' Wolf and Frank Sinatra, it was also the favourite piece of Bonnie and Clyde.

Stop And Listen Blues, which drew its inspiration from Tommy Johnson's "Big Road Blues" and included the seminal lines "smokestack lightning, shines like gold", was another triumph, though lesser-known cuts like Tell Me To Do Right and She's Crazy About Her Lovin' are even more poised. At their best the Sheiks centred on a beautifully balanced interplay between fiddle and guitar, though sometimes Vinson placed himself too deep in the shadows. On the other hand, Chatmon was capable of weaving magic single-handed, as with his flamboyant double-time runs at the end of each verse of The World Is Going Wrong.

In homage to country pioneer Jimmie Rodgers, certain Sheiks tracks feature his trademark "blue yodels". Rodgers had himself been influenced by the blues, and Bob Mills, the originator of "western swing", was in turn a fan of the Sheiks. To run the gamut a little further, Please Baby is a conventional pop croon, whereas Sweet Maggie became a folk standard as "Corrina, Corrina". At least Shooting High Dice is unequivocally blues, being sung to the tune of "St Louis Blues", while He Calls That Religion stands in the tradition of blues lampoons of corrupt clergymen, complete with the unsubtle tag line of "I know he's going to hell when he dies."

Lonnie Chatmon died not long after the Sheiks split up in 1935, but Walter Vinson made some solo recordings for Bluebird in Chicago in the early 1940s, and even revived the group once or twice with assorted other Chatmons before his death in 1975.

⮕ We almost chose **Complete Recorded Works Vol.1**, Document, 1994

68

Junior Parker

Mystery Train

Rounder, 1990; recorded 1953–54

If "the blues had a baby, and they named the baby rock and roll", then visitors to Memphis' Sun Studios in 1953 would have seen the blues looking very heavily pregnant indeed. Although Sam Phillips had started Sun as a blues label the year before, something new was emerging. In showcasing Junior Parker's two Sun singles, the **Mystery Train** CD captures a defining moment. It's probably the shortest CD in this book, only stretching to 38 minutes thanks to five unreleased outtakes and five more tracks by sidemen on which Parker doesn't even appear, but if any blues ranks as truly essential it's the four sides of those two singles.

Herman Parker was born in West Memphis, Arkansas, in 1932. By the age of 16, the fledgling harmonica player had inveigled his way into the band of his hero Sonny Boy Williamson II, where he was given the name "Little Junior". He also played with Howlin' Wolf, on tour and on his radio show, though not on Wolf's own sessions for Sun. Thanks to Ike Turner, he started recording under his own name for Modern Records in 1952.

The young Parker was a sophisticated blues balladeer, modelling himself on Nat "King" Cole and Johnny Ace, with a sideline as a soulful harpist. Neither talent came to the fore under Phillips' supervision at Sun. Instead, his first release, Feelin' Good – credited to "Little Junior And The Blue Flames", and cut in June 1953 – was a slice of exuberant country boogie.

Down to lifted lines like "last night I was laying in bed, I heard poppa and momma talking", it drew heavily on John Lee Hooker's 1948 "Boogie Chillen", using a whole lot more jive talk to fill the gaps before Parker whooped out the chorus again. Even if he doesn't quite sound like a teenager, there's a proto-rock'n'roll attitude there for perhaps the first time on record. Flip side **Fussin' And Fightin'** was a passionate, if more conventional, piano-based blues, complete with gentle sax solo.

The follow-up, recorded in the autumn of 1953, was the one that did it. Critic Robert Parker (no relation) called **Mystery Train** "the most metaphysically potent song in all of rock and roll", and certainly the mood amounts to much more than the narrative. The shuffling stream-train rhythm, the fluid guitar lines of Floyd Murphy and the jaunty piano form a seductive backdrop to Junior Parker's doleful vocals, to create a haunting overall impression that betrays the song's Celtic origins. Blues guitarists at the time were generally moving towards harder-edged amplified effects, and arguably the Sun sound – as also heard on the "black rockabilly" B-side, **Love My Baby** – represents a watering-down of pure blues for a crossover audience. At its best, however, it also created space amid the music for the star performer to shine through.

That Junior Parker's version of "Mystery Train" was not a hit hastened his departure to Peacock Records, where he became a major-league blues vocalist (see p.137). The offcuts and outtakes of his Sun years here add little to the story, although **Sittin' Drinkin' And Thinkin'** shows him working for the first time in tandem with guitarist Pat Hare, a more aggressive stylist. Hare also features as a solo artist on the furious **I'm Gonna Murder My Baby** – only released after he did just that in 1960 – and on James Cotton's searing **Cotton Crop Blues**, from May 1954. Cotton's limitations as a vocalist no doubt prompted Sam Phillips to start searching through his address book; the very next month, he called the young hopeful Elvis Presley back into the studio.

⊃ We almost chose **The Blues Came Down From Memphis**, Charly, 1998

69

Junior Parker

Junior's Blues: The Duke Recordings Vol.1

MCA, 1992; recorded 1953–64

Herman "Little Junior" Parker is best remembered as the man who almost invented rock'n'roll with his Sun recording of "Mystery Train". However, his heart was always in the blues, and after his brief Sun sojourn he went on to become one of the greatest blues vocalists. In fact, Parker was still signed to Sun when he passed through Houston en route to California early in 1954, and was persuaded by Don Robey to try his luck with Peacock Records instead. Sam Phillips sued Robey and won $17,500 – exactly half what RCA later paid him for Elvis – as well as half the copyright to "Mystery Train", which partly explains why Elvis re-recorded the song.

Robey also took over the Memphis-based Duke label, transferring its operations to Texas, and all the recordings Junior Parker made over the next thirteen years were released on Duke. They count as some of the finest blues vocal performances ever. The eighteen sides collected on **Junior's Blues** are just a small sample, but they make an ideal introduction to the work of a man whose reputation deserves to stand much higher.

As an instrument, Parker's voice never quite equalled that of his more celebrated stablemate, Bobby Bland – let alone that of his own cousin, Al Green – but his range of expression and timbre, and his skill at interpreting his material, were second to none. The backing he was given by the Duke house bands was also a constant delight, with ever-inventive horn arrangements blending swing, bebop and jazz atop a bedrock of solid Delta blues. Despite his ear for an attractive melody, Parker was always a grittier proposition than Bobby Bland; even on the cuts where his abrasive harp isn't given scope to let rip, there's always something tough and chewy in the mix.

Wild man guitarist Auburn "Pat" Hare made the move to Texas along with Parker, and for his first few Duke outings he pretty much picked up where he'd left off at Sun. The echoey I Wanna Ramble was another countrified boogie in the Hooker-esque mould of "Feelin' Good", and was in turn cut by John Lee Hooker in the early 1960s, while Sitting And Thinking was a rueful and slightly slicker remake of the Sun sessions' "Sittin' Drinkin' And Thinkin'".

Parker's first national hit for Duke, the swinging Next Time You See Me in 1956, was followed by the brooding ballad That's All Right. Among standards given the definitive Parker treatment over the next few years were Roosevelt Sykes' Driving Wheel – whose powerful horn phrases, heavily amped drums and call-and-response cries suggest how Parker and Bland's touring Blues Consolidated revue must have sounded – and Sweet Home Chicago. On Yonder's Wall, cut a couple of years after Elmore James' 1961 version, Junior relishes the lines, "Your husband's been to the war, I know it was tough, I don't know how many men he's killed, but I know he's done killed enough", while the horns are forced to make way for a fully fledged guitar solo. There's a similar electrifying tension to Percy Mayfield's Strange Things Happening, which has an eerie "Mystery Train" sort of ambience, and Parker's own In The Dark, in both of which his harp does lonely battle against the blaring brass. Gospel influences sneak in too, with his Little Richard yelps on the punchy Seven Days, and appeals of "can I get a witness?" at the end of It's A Pity.

Junior Parker lived only five more years after leaving Duke; he died while undergoing surgery for a brain tumour in November 1971, at the age of 39.

➲ We nearly chose **Backtracking: The Duke Recordings Vol.2**, MCA, 1998

70

Charlie Patton

Founder Of The Delta Blues

Yazoo, 1990; recorded 1929–34

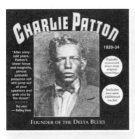

Even if Charlie Patton didn't "found" the Delta blues, there's a strong case for regarding Patton, rather than Robert Johnson, as its most important figure. Johnson after all was twenty years younger, and his recordings mark the end of the interwar heyday of acoustic country blues. Patton by contrast had been acknowledged as the premier exponent of the genre for well over a decade before he entered the Paramount studios in 1929. Johnson, it's true, was more "influential", in that his guitar innovations paved the way for the electrification of the blues. But the fact that Patton was less copied than Johnson might simply reflect the fact that what he did was more difficult.

Johnson is also known for the passionate intensity of his lyrics. No matter that he didn't so much write them as assemble them; they seemed to hint at mysteries deep within his soul. Patton's songs, on the other hand, are less personally revealing, and often barely coherent. His recordings can be hard to decipher: the sound quality tends to be extremely poor, while his gruff voice verges on the incomprehensible.

Patton's reputation rests on his consummate skills as a musician, as displayed across the 26 tracks of Yazoo's **Founder Of The Delta Blues**. A master of both bottleneck and finger-picking techniques, he was also a renowned showman. Son House, recalling such Patton antics as playing the guitar behind his head, sniffed that "he clowned too much". He was more than just a talented instrumentalist, however; his records are characterized above all by his unfailing ear for rhythm, as he stamped out complex patterns with his feet, banged them against the body of his guitar, or barked them in staccato bursts.

Born in the hills near Jackson, Mississippi, in 1887 or 1891, Charlie Patton moved to the Dockery Plantation around the turn of the century. The blues itself, and widespread use of the guitar, were then so new that it's impossible to know whether Patton picked up his style from music "traditional" to his community; was taught it by some unsung genius; or invented it himself. Certainly, he's recalled as having been playing his future classics by 1910, which doesn't allow much time for other people to have written them and passed them on.

Patton was a professional musician, playing barrelhouses and juke joints, for the rest of his life. He recorded his signature piece, Pony Blues, at his debut Paramount session in 1929. Graced by stunning interplay between voice and guitar, it's a virtuoso performance. Shake It And Break It is a lighter dance number, while Mississippi Bo Weavil Blues follows an archaic ballad structure of two-line verses. Howlin' Wolf grew up on Dockery's, and the young Willie Dixon was a neighbour, which explains why Banty Rooster Blues and A Spoonful Blues turned up as Chicago blues standards thirty years later. There's a Muddy Waters connection, too: the catchy Elder Green Blues and Going To Move To Alabama both feature the fiddle of Son Sims, who also played on Muddy's 1941 plantation recordings (see p.173).

High Water Everywhere, a dramatic two-part account of the 1927 Mississippi flood, was Patton's biggest seller. Paramount let him go in 1930, however, and by the time he recorded a further 29 sides in New York for Vocalion in 1934, his health was deteriorating. The fact that his throat had recently been cut did little for his voice. Nonetheless, his musical imagination remained strong, as displayed on remakes of Tom Rushen Blues as High Sherriff Blues and "Pony Blues" as Stone Pony Blues, and a duet with Bertha Lee, one of his reputed eight "wives", entitled "Oh Death". He was dead himself three months later.

➲ We almost chose **King Of The Delta Blues**, Yazoo, 1991

71

Washington Phillips

I Am Born To Preach The Gospel

Yazoo, 1992; recorded 1927–29

Less is probably known about Washington Phillips than any other musician featured in this book. All that can be stated with any certainty is that he made a total of eighteen recordings during his lifetime, over three successive Decembers in Dallas between 1927 and 1929. All have strong religious themes and, almost certainly, Phillips would have been horrified to find himself remembered as a blues singer rather than as a preacher.

While the parallels between Phillips and fellow Texan evangelist Blind Willie Johnson extend as far as recording the same song in the same week, Phillips' music is less readily identifiable. The reason for his inclusion is simple: you can argue as to whether he should be considered as blues, or gospel, or as an old-style "songster", but his songs are too hauntingly beautiful to be left out, as **I Am Born To Preach The Gospel** amply demonstrates.

No one even knows what instrument Phillips played, though it's generally called either a "dulceola" or a "dolceola". Neither word is in the dictionary, but the sound it made was every bit as sweet as the names suggest. According to Frank Walker, the Columbia engineer who recorded him, "He had no name for it; it was something he made himself. Nobody on earth could use it except him. Nobody would want to, I don't think." This peculiar contraption seems to have been some sort of zither or dulcimer, consisting of perhaps dozens of metal strings laid tight across a flat wooden frame. From the sound of it, Phillips both plucked chords and struck it with cloth-headed hammers; not surprisingly, there's a palpable sense of studied concentration during his more complex pieces.

While picking out heartbreaking tunes on the dulceola, which chimes away like a barrel organ or music box, Phillips declaims whatever gospel message may be on his mind. Often his pieces start with a formal spoken introduction; on **Train Your Child**, indeed, he delivers an entire "lecture" into the crackling void and only then plays an unrelated instrumental coda. Of the well-known gospel songs in his repertoire, both **Take Your Burden To The Lord And Leave It There** and **A Mother's Last Word To Her Daughter** were also recorded by Blind Willie Johnson. Phillips' earnest vocal style sounds frail in comparison to the ferocious growling of the more accomplished Johnson but he certainly matches his contemporary in terms of emotional intensity.

The most interesting material are the songs of Phillips wrote himself. Best known is the two-part **Denomination Blues**, in which to a constant refrain of "you better have Jesus, I tell you that's all" he first runs through potted summaries of the beliefs of various rival churches, and then turns his attention to the kind of preacher who "had to go to college to learn how to preach." The personal relevance of that theme is stressed in **I Am Born To Preach The Gospel** itself, in which he states "I have never been to no college, and I didn't get a chance in school." His masterpiece, however, is the almost unbearably poignant **I Had A Good Father And Mother**, in which he eulogizes his dead parents, castigates himself as an unworthy sinner, and thanks God for at least granting him the blessing of friends.

Blues scholars who scoured the registers of births and deaths in Phillips' hometown of Austin, Texas, found only one individual who matches his surmised dates. That Washington Phillips was born around 1891, which would put him in his late thirties at the time of these recordings. Poignantly, he seems to have been incarcerated in the State Hospital for the insane just a few months later, where he died, with no known family to claim his remains, on December 31, 1938.

➲ We almost chose **Storefront & Streetcorner Gospel**, Document, 1994

72

Elvis Presley

Sunrise

RCA, 1999; recorded 1953–55

Looking now at footage of the young Elvis Presley, he seems an impossibly alien creature. Even his backing band appear bemused by his outlandish appearance, his flamboyant clothes and his raw sexual energy. If it's hard enough to accept that he was a human being, to pigeonhole him as a blues singer might seem too restrictive for words. And yet Elvis didn't descend fully fledged from the skies. He was born and raised in the Deep South, so poor a piece of "white trash" that the segregation of the day failed to separate him from black culture. Eventually, he moved on, but there's no disputing that, as Howlin' Wolf insisted, and Elvis's most perceptive critics – Peter Guralnick and Greil Marcus – concurred, he "made his pull from the blues".

The aptly named **Sunrise** two-CD set documents the dawn of Elvis's career, starting with the legendary demo disc he cut at the age of 18 in July 1953. It was no coincidence that brought him to Sam Phillips' Memphis Recording Service; this was the studio used by B.B. King, Howlin' Wolf and Junior Parker, and the headquarters of the exclusively blues-oriented Sun Records. Elvis presented himself as a ballad merchant, performing My Happiness and That's When Your Heartaches Begin, with a mournful, hesitant slur.

Time passed, and Elvis found work as a truck driver. Then, in June 1954, Phillips invited him to make a commercial recording. Listening to Elvis flounder through a further slew of ballads, Phillips encouraged him to sing something he felt truly comfortable with. While Scotty Moore kept things simple on guitar, and Bill Black got slaphappy on his echoey stand-up bass, Elvis tore into **That's All Right** with a fresh, heady exhilaration far removed from the muted resignation of Arthur "Big Boy" Crudup's original 1946 hit.

No one knew how to define this new music. An acetate played over the radio before the record even existed made it a local smash. But was it black or white, blues or country? Phillips put a country song on the flip side, **Blue Moon Of Kentucky**, a formula he followed for every Elvis single thereafter. Suddenly, however, there was a new audience who didn't care; within days, teenagers were greeting each other on the streets of Memphis with the arcane cry "ta dee dah dee dee dah."

In retrospect, it's easy to forget that Elvis's Sun sessions were spread out over sixteen months, and to imagine that everything just fell into place. In fact, whatever the surface spontaneity, each new disc took endless crafting. Elvis didn't turn up knowing what he was going to record; instead, he trawled through his prodigious memory, assembling fragments and adding his own style and phrasing.

Though popular myth might have it that he "stole" from unsung black musicians, you only have to compare Elvis's charismatic slices of self-invention with such lacklustre originals as Arthur Gunter's **Baby Let's Play House** to realize that a creative genius was at work. Similarly, **Milkcow Blues Boogie** was credited to Kokomo Arnold, but had been cunningly melded with Bob Wills' "Brain Cloudy Blues" – and neither source would matter a hoot without that breathtaking stop-start intro, "Hold it fellas . . . let's get *real* gone for a change." Even when the originals had their own undoubted strengths, as with Junior Parker's **Mystery Train** and Roy Brown's **Good Rockin' Tonight**, Elvis transformed them. Subtle changes in the lyrics, and the lip-smacking relish of his intonation, turned world-weariness and all-too-adult boasting into epics of youthful exuberance and optimism. Even Elvis's day finally had to end; but, in the glory of his *Sunrise*, anything was possible.

➲ We almost chose **The Great Performances**, RCA, 1990

73

Professor Longhair

'Fess – The Professor Longhair Anthology

Rhino, 1993; recorded 1949–80

The breathtaking piano skills of Professor Longhair remained sadly underappreciated for most of his lifetime. Twenty years after his death, however, he lives on as the patron saint of New Orleans R&B. To his original grounding in the blues, he added a gorgeous gumbo of influences and a magical sense of inventiveness and play. The world of blues piano offers no greater pleasures than to luxuriate in the two-hour, two-CD extravaganza of Rhino's **'Fess – The Professor Longhair Anthology**.

Henry Roeland Byrd was two months old when he arrived in New Orleans at the start of 1919. He began by tap-dancing for tips on Bourbon Street before graduating to a scavenged broken-down piano. Following in the steps of role models like Kid Stormy Weather and Isidore "Tuts" Washington, he was soon a "professor" in his own right – the honorific was traditionally attached to the pianists of the city's bars and brothels.

Fronting "Professor Longhair And His Shuffling Hungarians", he evolved a unique personal style, characterized by flurries of ultra-fast triplets atop a steady rumba beat. The driving rhythms were boosted by percussive input from his right foot; sometimes he'd have a bass drum down there, sometimes a board, and sometimes he'd just kick the piano to pieces. One former bandmate spoke of "a Caribbean left hand and a boogie woogie right hand"; Jerry Wexler of Atlantic Records hailed him as "the Picasso of keyboard funk"; and he himself said his music consisted of "offbeat Spanish beats and Calypso downbeats."

Record companies first noticed Byrd in 1949. Mercury gave him his first and only national R&B hit with the comedy song Bald Head in 1950, though it was Fats Domino whose "flying triplets" captured the mass market soon afterwards. The first true Longhair masterpiece came in 1953, when Atlantic released Tipitina. Powered by the "second-line" drumming of Earl Palmer, it's been one of the great party records in New Orleans ever since, but 'Fess' extraordinary Pig Latin jive-talk yodelling – all that "Tra la oh la mala walla" – was too downright weird for the charts. Go To The Mardi Gras has become an equally durable carnival anthem; the version here is his third and definitive 1959 recording, with Dr John on guitar.

For most of the 1960s, health and legal problems forced Longhair to abandon music altogether. 1964, however, saw perhaps his finest achievement: the intoxicating Big Chief. Written and sung by Earl King, it's blessed by the most astonishing, supple, hypnotic piano riff ever invented; couple that with a barrage of brass arranged by Wardell Quezergue, and you have a sublime work of art.

All these early classics appear on the first disc of 'Fess. The second is devoted to the 1970s, after Byrd was "rediscovered" by blues enthusiasts. As well as seven tracks from Rock'N'Roll Gumbo, featuring Clarence "Gatemouth" Brown, there are two from Crawfish Fiesta, with Snooks Eaglin. The real joys, however, are the live tracks, recorded in 1978 at Tipitina's, the club set up to give him a regular venue. Blues standards like Everyday I Have The Blues and Got My Mojo Working are performed with the Blues Scholars, while on the lovely Rum & Coca Cola he's backed by a subtle conga player alone. Recognition came too late: Longhair died in 1980, two weeks after he recorded Boogie Woogie and two days before a major showcase concert. As Dr John put it, "before him was the void; after him, we're just whistling in the dark."

➲ We almost chose **Crawfish Fiesta**, Alligator, 1987

74

Ma Rainey

Ma Rainey's Black Bottom

Yazoo, 1991; recorded 1924–28

The 93 songs that Gertrude "Ma" Rainey cut for the Paramount label between 1923 and 1928 date from the very dawn of the recording industry. At the time, they were seen as harking back to an even earlier era. Paramount promoted her first release with the slogan "Discovered at last – 'Mother of the Blues'", but dropped her altogether by the end of the decade because her style was regarded as too antiquated to sell. It's extraordinary, therefore, just how fresh, vigorous and characterful the fourteen tracks of Yazoo's beautifully restored **Ma Rainey's Black Bottom** sound almost eighty years on. That's partly because blues and jazz had yet to go their separate ways, and the backing provided by an array of early jazz greats is a delight in its own right. Credit is largely due, however, to the undimmed personality of Ma Rainey herself.

Born in 1886 in Columbus, Georgia, Gertrude Pridgett became "Ma" at the tender age of 18, when she married the less talented William "Pa" Rainey, a comedian whose act consisted of stuffing a saucer in his mouth. That same year, she joined him on tour with the Rabbit Foot Minstrels. One night in Missouri, a young woman came to their tent after a show and sang a strange mournful song, which "Ma" swiftly incorporated into her act. She later claimed to have invented the word "blues" to describe this new music. Billed as "Rainey And Rainey: Assassinators Of The Blues", the couple spent the next dozen summers on the vaudeville circuit, and wintered in

New Orleans, where they hooked up with the likes of Louis Armstrong.

Ma Rainey then established her own touring company, and had acquired a huge following by the time she came to record. She struck an especial chord among women: contrary to the popular stereotype, very few of her songs portray women as downtrodden victims, and not one contains a positive mention of marriage. More often glad to be free of her man than bereft without him, she celebrated sexual freedom, with occasional explicit lesbian references (as on "Prove It On Me Blues"). She was renowned both for her ostentatious, exuberant displays – she'd shimmy on stage from within a giant gramophone, festooned with sequins and diamonds – and the forthright robustness of her lyrics.

There's probably no better-known double entendre in the blues than her signature tune, Ma Rainey's Black Bottom itself. Strictly speaking, the black bottom was a dance, but with lines like "Ma Rainey is gonna show you her black bottom" and "all the boys in the neighborhood, say your black bottom's really good", it's impossible not to feel there's something else going on as well. The jaunty Shave 'Em Dry is another commanding vocal performance, while Yonder Comes The Blues is altogether more serious in its chilling Robert Johnson-esque depiction of the blues as a palpable, malevolent entity.

The musical accompaniment is varied and enjoyable throughout, with nine distinct line-ups at work. Both Oh Papa Blues and Blues Oh Blues, from 1927, showcase Kid Ory on trombone, with gorgeous bass-lines from an uncredited tuba, while Black Eye Blues and Sleep Talking Blues boast Tampa Red on guitar and Georgia Tom on piano. The much-recorded Stack O' Lee Blues, which has Coleman Hawkins on bass sax, is intriguing in that the tune is in fact that equally well-known chestnut, "Frankie And Albert", while the lyrics are a hybrid of the two songs, complete with "he was her man, and he doin' her wrong."

➲ We almost chose **Ma Rainey**, Milestone, 1992

75

Jimmy Reed

The Masters

Eagle Records, 1998; recorded 1953–64

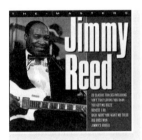

Despite the simplicity of his blues recipe, not only did Jimmy Reed have an unmatched degree of chart success during his lifetime, but his work still sounds immediately recognizable, and utterly characterful, 25 years after his death. Even after countless covers and imitations, Reed has never been bettered. In fact he was an inspiration to younger musicians precisely because his music required so little technical proficiency, and because the lazy charm of his singing made the process of attaining stardom appear so effortless. His output at his peak was so consistent that while the many compilations of his hits tend to differ by a few tracks, there's no significant variation in quality. **The Masters** is no more definitive than the others, but has the advantage of delivering twenty songs at a budget price.

Born in Mississippi in September 1925, Jimmy Reed moved to Chicago 1943, and eventually found a job in a meat-packing plant in Gary, Indiana. There he teamed up with his boyhood friend Eddie Taylor, who had taught him to play guitar back home, and who always remained streets ahead of him as a guitarist. Following an unsuccessful audition for Chess – who long rued their failure to spot his potential – he moved to Vee Jay Records in 1953, on the recommendation of Albert King.

It took three singles on Vee Jay to establish the trademark Reed style. His slurred vocals, modelled on his little-known predecessor "Mushmouth" Robinson, coasted atop a gentle boogie propelled by the "walking bass" lines of Taylor's rhythm guitar, and were interspersed by perfunctory blasts of the harp Reed wore on a rack around his neck. Although there was little room for improvisation, the boogie itself was innovative, and cited as an influence by Chuck Berry among others. Reed's third release, **You Don't Have To Go**, kicked off a run of fourteen R&B and eleven pop chart entries. Over the next ten years, he far outsold giants like Muddy Waters and John Lee Hooker, even if he never saw nearly as much money as that might suggest.

The most crucial element in Reed's success was the contribution of his wife Mary Lee "Mama" Reed – a contribution not fully appreciated at the time. Not only did she write virtually all the lyrics (at times in the studio itself), but she ensured that Jimmy, who couldn't read, didn't even have to learn them. Most songs were recorded in one take, with Mama Reed either mouthing each line to him just before he sang it, or coaxing him all the way through. You can hear her voice, for example, on the classic **Bright Lights, Big City**; she's not so much accompanying him as prompting him.

Jimmy Reed's strong performance in the pop charts, at a time when that was unsusual for black artists in general, let alone bluesmen, had a lot to do with the entirely unthreatening, almost asexual, tone of his voice and his material. That in turn stemmed in part from the input of Mama Reed. Several of the songs have been covered by women such as Etta James and Tina Turner, who on **Honest I Do** told Ike, "you're the sweetest little *man* that I ever had."

Sadly, Reed's problems with alcohol, exacerbated by his epilepsy, made him unable to build on the international reputation he achieved with such standout tracks as **Baby What You Want Me To Do**, **Hush Hush** and **Big Boss Man**. After Eddie Taylor went solo in 1965, the hits dried out, but Reed himself didn't. He continued to record intermittently, with dire results, until his death in California in 1976.

➲ We almost chose **Big Boss Man**, Snapper, 1999

76

The Rolling Stones

The Rolling Stones

ABKCO, 1987; recorded 1963–64

The notion of bratty middle-class white kids trying to play the blues is so familiar these days that it's hard to remember that the Rolling Stones changed everything. In 1964, however, the idea of anyone playing the blues to make money had become absurd; after all, when the Stones made the pilgrimage to Chess during their first visit to the States that year, they found Muddy Waters dressed in overalls and painting the studio.

That American tour came hard on the heels of the release of their first album, **The Rolling Stones – England's Newest Hit Makers**. To include a Stones album in a book of essential blues CDs might seem questionable now, but when they started out the band saw themselves as blues purists. Inspired by the urban blues of Chicago, and named after a Waters song, their sole aim was to reproduce the Chess sound in all its murky majesty.

All kinds of factors conspired to turn the Stones' genuflection into genius. The first was that in their raw enthusiasm they brought so many flavours to the pot; they loved Chuck Berry as much as Muddy Waters, and relished the pop sensibilities of Motown. Second – whatever their dreams – they couldn't help but remain British, distanced from their sources and obliged to fill the gaps with guesswork. On top of that, they had the Beatles to react against, and so cast themselves as scruffy tearaways. Finally, they were also talented musicians, blessed with a consummately swinging rhythm section in Bill Wyman and Charlie Watts, and adorned by Brian Jones' prodigious mimicry of slide guitar and harmonica stylings. And that's not to mention Mick Jagger and Keith Richards.

The Rolling Stones is not the group's best album, and they even produced plenty of more accomplished blues covers later in their career (such as "Little Red Rooster", "Love In Vain" and "Shake Your Hips", to name but three). It was, however, a defining moment in blues history. From the insouciant sub-two-minute swagger of the Bo-Diddley-fied Not Fade Away to the exuberant barking of Walking The Dog, it crammed the blueprint for a revolution into just over half an hour.

The crucial track here is I'm A King Bee, a blues standard that goes all the way back to Bo Carter and Memphis Minnie. The Stones modelled their version on the gloriously ramshackle cut that had kick-started Slim Harpo's career in 1957. Centred on the equally anarchic interplay between Jones' slide guitar and Richards' fuzzy buzzing, it proved a perfect platform for Jagger's teen-rebel posturings. In his desperation to sound "authentic", he came out instead with enough adenoidal adolescent angst to capture the hearts of a generation. Defusing the adult sexuality of Muddy's I Just Want To Make Love To You, and turning it into a pop anthem, may not have been the goal, but as a piece of art it was no less "true" than the original.

Sonny Boy Williamson II famously said of the British blues bands that "they want to play the blues so bad – and they play it so *bad*." Whatever else they may have been, the Rolling Stones were not bad; Jimmy Reed's Honest I Do, powered along by the thumping drums of Charlie Watts, proves they could deliver the goods. Andrew Loog Oldham's endearing sleeve notes assess their achievements "in the eight months since the Stones embarked on their pop career." You might not like what they did with it in the end, but when they first got their teeth into the blues, the Stones tore it apart.

⊃ We almost chose **Singles Collection – The London Years**, ABKCO, 1989

77

Bessie Smith

The Collection

Columbia, 1989; recorded 1923–33

Forever remembered as the "Empress of the Blues", Bessie Smith remains the biggest star the music has ever known. Before the Depression brought the Jazz Age to an end, she captivated black and white audiences alike with her rough-hewn persona, indomitable spirit and spellbinding voice. As demonstrated on this budget compilation, **The Collection**, she was accompanied by the era's greatest sidemen, although she was more than capable of handling things on her own.

The blues' first superstar was born in Chattanooga, Tennessee, in 1894, and orphaned at the age of 8. After an apprenticeship singing on the streets, she joined her brother Clarence in 1912 in Moses Stokes' entertainment troupe, and came under the wing of Gertrude "Ma" Rainey. That may have been her first exposure to the blues, but claims that Rainey taught her to sing do little justice to her awesome natural talents.

Smith's first chance to record came in 1923, in the wake of Mamie Smith's success with "Crazy Blues". She was more than ready. Her debut, a cover of Alberta Hunter's Downhearted Blues, sold 780,000 copies in six months. Two months later, she cut another classic, Porter Grainger's Tain't Nobody's Bizness If I Do. Though Columbia paid her a paltry $200 per side, she was soon commanding $2000 per week as a live attraction.

The undoubted highlight here is a collaboration rarely (if ever) surpassed in popular music – the January 1925 acoustic session that paired Smith with the young Louis Armstrong. Her every vocal inflection on the definitive Saint Louis Blues is perfectly complemented by Armstrong's cornet, while Fred Longshaw pumps his harmonium like a steamboat calliope. Reckless Blues and You've Been A Good Ole Wagon from the same day are touched with an equal magic.

Elsewhere, two of Bessie's own songs stand out. Young Woman's Blues is a sassy assertion of her independence: "I ain't no high yellow, I'm a deep killer brown, I ain't gonna marry, ain't gon' settle down." Empty Bed Blues, by contrast, consists of a hilarious string of deadpan double entendres – "he's a deep-sea diver, with a stroke that can't go wrong, he can touch the bottom, and his will holds out so long" – punctuated by playful blasts from Charlie Green's trombone. Lonnie Johnson's Mean Old Bedbug Blues is a similar delight, graced with stately Latinate guitar flourishes from Lincoln Conaway.

Smith's last hit, the compelling Nobody Knows You When You're Down And Out, was cut in May 1929, the night after her Broadway debut in the revue *Pansy*. Despite her acclaimed performance, the show was panned and closed almost immediately. The song proved prophetic: the Wall Street Crash came five months later, destroying not only record sales but also the live theatrical circuit on which Smith depended.

Columbia declined to renew Smith's contract after 1931. On John Hammond's insistence, and against her protests that "nobody wants to hear blues no more" – borne out by the fact that she was now working for tips in a gin mill – she cut four sides for OKeh in 1933. All written by vaudeville duo Coot Grant and Kid Sock Wilson, and cut with a band that included Jack Teagarden on trombone and Benny Goodman on clarinet, songs such as Do Your Duty and Gimme A Pigfoot offer a fascinating glimpse of what she might have become in the swing era. By a sad irony, Bessie's life ended in Clarksdale, Mississippi – the birthplace of so many blues greats – following a car crash on September 26, 1937. The legend that she died after being refused admission to a whites-only hospital has long been discredited.

⮑ We almost chose **The Essential Bessie Smith**, Columbia, 1997

78

Pops Staples

Peace To The Neighborhood

Pointblank, 1992

Considering his credentials – as a child he was taught to play guitar by Charlie Patton on Will Dockery's plantation in the Mississippi Delta – it took Roebuck "Pops" Staples a very long time to make his first solo album. When he recorded **Peace To The Neighborhood** in 1992, the patriarch of the Staples Singers was 77 years old. As he put it, "I said when I was about twelve years old that I was going to make a record one of these days. So I got singing and then all of the family jumped in on me and I had to take them to sing. Well, that flooded my part out for about sixty years. But I never gave up . . ."

Whether Pops really counts as a blues artist is debatable, but this book is happy to follow the lead of the Grammy awards committee, which hailed *Father, Father*, the follow-up to *Peace To The Neighborhood*, as the Best Contemporary Blues Album of 1995. There's no disputing that word "contemporary", however, even though Pops had by then passed 80. Whether you call his music gospel, soul or blues, it has always served as the vehicle for a message, from the explicit social protest of the Staples Singers' involvement in the Civil Rights movement to the more broadly uplifting themes of their chart-topping period with Stax in the 1970s. *Peace To The Neighborhood* carried on that same tradition, given an added urgency and authority by the fact that it might well stand as Staples' final testament.

In some respects *Peace To The Neighborhood* is little different to a Staples Singers album. Pops' three daughters, Mavis, Yvonne and Cleotha, appear on three tracks, and Mavis even takes the lead vocal on **Pray On My Child**. Most important of all – and the first thing any prospective listener will want to know – is that Pops' utterly distinctive guitar sounds the same as ever, drenched in reverb and echoing richly through the bottom of the mix. This delicious tone created an immediate impact from its first airing in the early 1950s, influencing Curtis Mayfield among others (he later returned the favour by signing the Staples to his Custom label after they left Stax), but there's still no one who does it better. It's only absent on one track – oddly enough, the title song, **Peace To The Neighborhood** – and there it's sorely missed.

Although *Peace To The Neighborhood* is very much a product of its time in the way it uses guest rock stars to give it crossover appeal, Staples remains the commanding presence. On **World In Motion**, the opening track, his playing is beautifully complemented by the guitars of Bonnie Raitt and Jackson Browne, and only when they join in the singing does the spell get broken. The two cuts that feature Ry Cooder are exceptional; despite Staples' Delta roots, his playing focuses on lushly textured bass runs, so Cooder's spiky slide contributions to **I Shall Not Be Moved** and **Down In Mississippi** are a real pleasure.

More than half the album was recorded in Memphis, as opposed to Los Angeles, with Willie Mitchell serving as Pops' co-producer on four tracks. The standout here is **America**, a funky state-of-the-nation address adorned by the sassy phrasings of Wayne Jackson and Andrew Love, the Memphis Horns. Best of all, however, are Pops' two self-produced gems: **This May Be The Last Time**, a stately rereading of the Staples' classic (as filched by the Rolling Stones), and **Miss Cocaine**, a dark, passionate sermon on the perils of addiction.

⊃ We almost chose **Jammed Together**, Stax, 1969

79

Tampa Red

The Guitar Wizard

Columbia, 1994; recorded 1928–34

Tampa Red was the most prolific of the early bluesmen. During his thirty-year career, he cut well over three hundred solo sides in the 78 rpm format alone, as well as backing singers such as Ma Rainey and Victoria Spivey. He's mostly celebrated as a bottleneck guitarist but he also played piano and kazoo and, though never the most expressive of singers, popularized some of the blues' most classic songs. To modern ears the acoustic recordings on **The Guitar Wizard** may sound typical of prewar country blues, but even at that stage of his career Tampa Red was closely associated with Chicago and ranks among the most important of the pioneers who turned the blues into an urban art form.

Born Hudson Woodbridge in rural Georgia, around 1904, Tampa Red acquired both his nickname and his adult surname of Whittaker from the grandmother who raised him in Tampa, Florida. By the mid-1920s, he was making his living as a musician in Chicago, with a guitar style shaped more by the popular songs of the day than by the blues alone. Hawaiian guitarists in particular were a major influence on his delicate, precise bottleneck sound. Indeed, he later recalled that when he first teamed up with pianist Georgia Tom Dorsey "we didn't want to call ourselves blues singers." Instead they classified their music as "hokum", and recorded risqué, ragtime novelty numbers bursting with double entendres. Some numbers they'd chant more or less in unison, but often they left the singing to someone else.

Tight Like That, with vocals by female impersonator

Frankie Half Pint Jaxon, was an instant smash in 1928 – so much so that the duo produced a quick-fire succession of all but identical cuts within days of each other. Georgia Tom's heart really lay with gospel music, but an initial royalty cheque for $2400.19 persuaded him to stick with Tampa Red for another four years, as the Hokum Boys.

"Tight Like That" features on *The Guitar Wizard* not in the hit version but in one with Papa Too Sweet on vocals. An even more enjoyable hokum track is Dead Cats On The Line, a sassy chronicle of the infidelities of upright Chicago churchgoers: "You're brown-skinned, your husband ain't fair, Your children all yellow and got curly hair, There's a dead cat on the line." Others, like You Can't Get That Stuff No More, could be taken as referring equally to alcohol or sex.

Following the split from Georgia Tom, who turned to full-time gospel – with colossal success – in 1932, Tampa Red underwent a change of direction. Turpentine Blues in particular is a Depression-era saga of hard times that's entirely devoid of the broad humor characterizing the Hokum Boys' output. However, Tampa Red was above all an accomplished professional musician rather than a tortured artist. Thus Things 'Bout Comin' My Way lacks the passion of Robert Johnson's subsequent reworking "Come On In My Kitchen" – the melody of both songs deriving from the Mississippi Sheiks' 1930 recording of "Sitting On Top Of The World". Another song here, Black Angel Blues, similarly formed the template for the B.B. King hit of the 1950s.

In the late 1930s and early 1940s, Tampa Red's Chicago home served as a way station for countless musicians arriving from the South – including Muddy Waters – and also as an informal audition space for Lester Melrose's Bluebird label. Red himself even had an R&B hit in 1949 with "It Hurts Me Too", a song Elmore James later made his own. Though he lived on until 1981, Tampa Red was too ill to record after 1960, and sadly failed to benefit from the subsequent blues revival.

➲ We almost chose **It Hurts Me Too**, Indigo, 1994

80

Hound Dog Taylor

Hound Dog Taylor And The HouseRockers

Alligator, 1989; recorded 1971

Thirty years ago, the House-Rockers already seemed like relics of a bygone era. The quintessential Chicago bar band appeared destined to play out their days in the backstreets of the Windy City. No record label saw their low-rent, no-frills, good-time boogie as having the slightest commercial appeal in the sophisticated 1970s. Bruce Iglauer, however, an employee of the Delmark company, was sufficently impressed to start his own label, specifically in order to record their first album. The unexpected success of **Hound Dog Taylor And The HouseRockers** not only gave Hound Dog himself a brief but heady dose of late-life acclaim, but launched Alligator Records as the major blues imprint of the next three decades.

By 1971 Hound Dog Taylor had been established in Chicago for almost thirty years, having moved north from Natchez, Mississippi, in his mid-twenties. In that time, he'd gravitated from playing on the streets to nonstop gigging in tiny clubs, and welded together the tight trio known as the HouseRockers. They didn't play typical Chicago blues: their sound was much closer to the furious down-South boogie of Hound Dog's mentor, Elmore James. Uniquely, Taylor's slashing slide guitar riffs were backed not by the usual rhythm section of bass and drums but by Brewer Phillips as a second guitarist, with Ted Harvey underpinning both on drums. As the mood took him, Phillips would sometimes play loping runs on the bass strings, sometimes he'd chop out rhythmic chord progressions, and sometimes, memorably, he'd battle Taylor head-on with his own solos. The HouseRockers used every trick in the book to boost their volume, cranking up their amplifiers until they throbbed and howled with distortion. Their ability as a threesome to render any room awash with noise enabled them to undercut all competition and guarantee steady work.

At the age of 56, Taylor had just two obscure singles to his name, and was ready to grab his last chance for the limelight. For his part, Iglauer's aim was to give the studio sessions the feel of just another HouseRockers gig, so they'd forget their surroundings and let their instinctive interplay run free. Far more tracks were recorded than could be used, and few retakes and no overdubbing the odd feedback screech or bum note was bound to sneak through. Overall, however, the band was on blistering form. Taylor cut loose on his cheap Japanese guitar, excitedly shrieking out high-pitched fragments of vocals atop Phillips' punchy power chords and Harvey's galloping drums.

From the opening She's Gone to the final thrash of 55th Street Boogie, the frenetic pace barely falters for an instant. The best ensemble pieces here are the extraordinarily fuzz-laden I Just Can't Make It, and their hysterical on-stage showstopper, Give Me Back My Wig. Not surprisingly, however, Taylor hits his absolute peak as a slide guitarist on the two songs most closely associated with Elmore James, Wild About You, Baby and It Hurts Me Too. Even the two instrumentals on which Phillips was formally assigned the lead role – 44 Blues, a reworking of Howlin' Wolf's "Forty Four", and the slightly slower Phillips' Theme – exude every drop as much raw energy as the rest.

Sadly, despite the demand, the HouseRockers' canon never grew to any great size. Alligator released a couple more studio albums and an official live set, and further live recordings have surfaced over the years. Theodore Roosevelt Taylor himself, however, only had four years to enjoy his new-found status before he died of cancer, aged 60, in December 1975.

➲ We almost chose **Deluxe Edition**, Alligator, 1999

81

Koko Taylor

What It Takes

Chess, 1991; recorded 1964–72

Though Koko Taylor's recordings for Chess proved to be the foundation of a long career, at the time she seemed to be something of an anachronism, as Chess had all but given up on out-and-out blues by the mid-1960s. While the old guard were still making new albums, albeit under constant pressure to adapt to changing times, as a rough-hewn new blues artist Koko was a rare breed indeed.

Raised on a farm outside Memphis, Cora Walton moved to Chicago with her husband Robert "Pops" Taylor in 1954, at the age of 18. It took almost ten years of scuffling before she hooked up with bassman, songwriter and entrepreneur Willie Dixon. Another ten years created the body of work collected on **What It Takes**. Of its eighteen tracks, Dixon is credited as composer of all but two, and producer of all but one. Dixon clearly recognized a kindred spirit in Taylor. He later recalled her telling him, "I can sing but every time I go to somebody and sing, they tell me they don't like this growl, that heavy part of my voice." Dixon loved it, relishing the chance to work with a female counterpart, in both singing style and sheer presence, to the likes of Howlin' Wolf.

Koko's first session for Chess, in June 1964, resulted in what remains her signature tune. I Got What It Takes was blessed with a stellar cast, with Buddy Guy and Robert Nighthawk trading licks on guitar, Clifton James slapping away at the drum kit, and "Big Walter" Horton providing delicate shading and an awesome solo on harp. Taylor, however, is the star from the word go, holding nothing back as she announces that she's the woman who's been reducing all those hard-bitten bluesmen to jelly for so many years.

It was Wang Dang Doodle from later that same year, however, that became the last Chess blues single to hit the charts, and made Taylor an overnight sensation. Howlin' Wolf's earlier version had gone largely unnoticed, and Dixon had to use all his powers of persuasion to overcome Taylor's insistence that "That ain't no song for a woman to sing." She's been at pains ever since to point out that she'd never heard of such a preposterous panoply of lowlifes as "butcher-knife totin' Annie, fast talkin' Fannie" and the rest. It's still a fabulous record, though, thanks to Buddy Guy's chiming guitar riffs and her own incandescent vocal.

Willie Dixon didn't always hit such lofty heights, but he could be depended upon for such catchy and witty blues material as Don't Mess With The Messer and What Came First The Egg Or The Hen. An unexpected joy here is Insane Asylum, a campy spoof on "St James Infirmary", with Dixon himself hamming it up à la Screaming Jay Hawkins – one of the rare occasions when his monotonous voice worked to his advantage.

Some of the punch goes from *What It Takes* following Buddy Guy's departure from Chess in 1967, but it winds up with a delightful live reprise of "I Got What It Takes", drawn from the 1972 Montreux Jazz Festival. This time it's a six-minute duet with Muddy Waters, plus a rhythm section comprised of Little Walter's former Aces. Verses from Muddy's own "The Same Thing" alternate with Koko's contributions, emphasizing how much the two songs have in common both with each other and with the standard "Spoonful".

When Koko Taylor left Chess shortly afterwards, she stayed with Willie Dixon on his short-lived Yambo label. By 1975, however, she was with Alligator Records, for whom she has been recording successfully ever since, with her band Blues Machine.

⊃ We almost chose **I Got What It Takes**, Alligator, 1991

82

Henry Thomas

Texas Worried Blues

Yazoo, 1989; recorded 1927–29

Born to recently freed slaves in east Texas in 1874, Henry Thomas was probably the earliest black musician to leave a significant body of recorded work. While he was first recorded in 1927, at the age of 53, both his style and repertoire are thought to date back to his early adulthood, and thus he provides a glimpse of secular black music in its earliest known form. Only four or five of his 23 recordings – all collected on Yazoo's **Texas Worried Blues: Complete Recorded Works 1927–29** – can really be called blues, and several are barely even songs at all, being uptempo square-dance tunes accompanied by random quick-fire "calls" and vocal impressions. However, taken together they offer an intriguing picture of the range of black popular music as the blues was taking shape.

Thomas was a "songster" rather than a blues singer. Before the widespread ownership of phonographs, he made his living as a human jukebox, performing popular songs for rent at dances and church picnics, and for tips on street corners. An inveterate hobo, recalled by a sympathetic railroad conductor as a "great big fellow", he travelled as far as Chicago for the Columbian Exhibition (1893) and St Louis for the World Fair (1904).

In his instrumentation, Thomas is very much a nineteenth-century figure, rhythmically strumming his guitar like a banjo while carrying his simple melodies alternately by singing and by blowing on a set of panpipes. Such pipes or "quills", cut from river reeds, were the common toys of rural children, but

Thomas is almost alone in having played them on disc. To modern ears, they give his music an appealingly crisp, fresh quality, even if he does swiftly run out of permutations of their scant five notes (it's easy to see why they were supplanted by the harmonica). Musicologists suggest that this sound harks back to the "whooping" of the Bantu peoples of the Congo/Angola region of Africa, many of whom were carried as slaves up the Mississippi River.

The vaudeville or Tin Pan Alley roots of much of Thomas's material indicates that his audience was often white, though no one knows quite how typical he was of contemporary black musicians in that respect. There's a strong impression that these are songs he has performed many times – some, such as **John Henry**, already seem so old as to be virtually devoid of meaning – and his gruff, inexpressive voice seldom hints at any great personal involvement. Several songs have been bowdlerized at the expense of all sense, presumably at the suggestion of his producers; **Arkansas**, for example, is closely based on a song called "Let Me Bring My Clothes Back Home", but substitutes "I'm done with beans, I'm gonna pass for green" for the original line, "I'm tired o' coon, I goin' to pass for white."

And yet listening to Thomas for the first time is like striking paydirt in the raw, rich, Texas soil, a mother lode that has been mined repeatedly and inexhaustibly ever since. Classic blues couplets glisten amid even the most mundane reels, while tunes such as **Don't Ease Me In** and **Don't You Leave Me Here** (both variations of the standard generally known as "Alabama Bound") and **Run Mollie Run** (now recognizable in the jazz staple "Li'l Liza Jane") boast an irresistible immediacy.

Future generations were quick to spot the commercial potential in Thomas's work. His catchiest song, **Bull Doze Blues**, based around a delightful melody on the quills, became a chart-topper for Canned Heat in the 1960s as "Goin' Up The Country", while Taj Mahal covered **Fishing Blues**, and Bob Dylan reworked **Honey, Won't You Allow Me One More Chance**.

⮞ We almost chose **Sings The Texas Blues**, Origin, 1991

83

Big Mama Thornton

Hound Dog: The Peacock Recordings

MCA, 1992; recorded 1952–57

Big Mama Thornton is one of those unfortunate musicians who's far more often name-checked for the people she influenced than she's actually listened to. Better-known singers not only adopted her characteristic blues-belting style, but they even appropriated her material. What Elvis did in the 1950s with "Hound Dog" Janis Joplin repeated a decade later with "Ball And Chain". Thornton herself, meanwhile, enjoyed little commercial success, and died lonely and embittered. As **Hound Dog: The Peacock Recordings** shows, her finest hour came at the dawn of her recording career.

Willie Mae Thornton left her home in Montgomery, Alabama, as a teenager in the early 1940s. On the road with Sammy Green's Hot Harlem Revue, she was groomed as a blues shouter in the mould of Bessie Smith, and learned to play both harmonica (from Junior Parker) and drums. In 1948, after an engagement in Houston, Texas, she decided to stay behind and work the city's club circuit. There she came to the attention of notorious local entrepreneur Don Robey, who signed her to Peacock Records in 1951.

After Thornton's initial sessions for Peacock, in Houston, bore little fruit, Robey decided to record her in Los Angeles instead, with Johnny Otis's band. *Hound Dog* features seven tracks cut in a single memorable day – August 13, 1952. All are gems, none more so than *Hound Dog* itself. Although Otis' entire orchestra was present, the sound for that one song was pared right down, to enhance its "country" feel. Backed by just three musicians – Pete Lewis carried the tune on guitar, while Albert Winston played bass, and Otis contributed simple slaps on the drums – Big Mama roared and growled her way to a #1 R&B hit. Both Otis and Thornton later claimed to have rewritten the song in the studio, but the courts eventually assigned full credit to the young team of Leiber and Stoller. The reason it became an issue was Elvis's multi-million-selling version in 1956. As a woman's song, with Thornton pouring scorn on the randy male dog scratching around her door and "wagging his tail", it might seem a strange number for Elvis to sing, but despite desexualizing the words, he beefed up the music considerably, turning Thornton's light rumba beat into serious rock'n'roll.

For the rest of that session, Johnny Otis moved to vibes and brought in his full horn section. As well as announcing herself on They Call Me Big Mama (if anything she weighed more than the three hundred pounds she claims here) Thornton delivered a couple of excellent slow blues, Walking Blues and I've Searched The Whole World Over. They also cut two more Leiber and Stoller numbers, including the ominous Nightmare, her phrasing on which was surely an inspiration to labelmate Bobby Bland.

Try as they might, Peacock never managed a second Thornton hit. Efforts included Yes, Baby in 1953, a duet with the ill-starred Johnny Ace (she was present when he died playing Russian roulette in a Houston theatre on Christmas Eve, 1954). From 1955 onwards, she recorded back in Houston with the Billy Harvey Orchestra, but whether she went for catchy dance numbers like The Fish, or powerful swing blues like How Come, nothing caught the public imagination.

Thornton eventually left Peacock on sour terms in 1957, claiming that Robey had cheated her of her due reward. A familiar figure on the festival circuit through the 1960s and 1970s, when she regularly performed wearing men's clothing, she cut some strong albums for the Arhoolie label. She died in Los Angeles in 1984.

➲ We almost chose **Ball N'Chain**, Arhoolie, 1990

84

Ali Farka Toure

Talking Timbuktu

World Circuit, 1994

It's impossible to say to what extent the blues "came from Africa." Musicologists have yet to agree what was happening in America at the end of the nineteenth century, just before W.C. Handy and Ma Rainey heard this strange new music for the first time, let alone trace the blues back to West Africa before the slave ships arrived. And yet tantalizing echoes and parallels abound. During the 1960s and 1970s, researchers like Samuel Charters and Paul Oliver released field recordings made in Africa that seemed at times uncannily close to the blues. In the 1980s and 1990s, blues artists such as Johnny Copeland and Taj Mahal returned the compliment, touring the continent and recording with African musicians.

With the rise of "world music", the voices of Africa have been increasingly heard in their own right. None has proved more fascinating than that of Ali Farka Toure, a farmer from Mali known as the "bluesman of Africa". Though making music is normally the preserve of certain castes in Malian society, Toure describes being granted the gift by a spirit in the night, as a 13-year-old in 1952 (a story that mirrors Robert Johnson's midnight visitation at a lonely Delta crossroads). Each of Toure's first instruments had a single string – the *djerkel*, plucked like a guitar, and the *njarka*, bowed like a violin. He acquired his first guitar on a visit to Bulgaria in 1968, which was also the year he encountered the blues.

Hearing records by Ray Charles and Otis Redding in the Malian capital Bamako was a revelation, but it was the rhythmic, repetitive groove of John Lee Hooker that made the greatest impression: "I thought he was Malian because of what I heard. It was one hundred percent our music." To be more specific, out of the many different styles of Malian music, Hooker's boogie reminded Toure of the Tamasheck sound of the nomadic Tuaregs, and the Bambara rhythms of the Peuls.

Toure spent the 1970s broadcasting on Radio Mali, before returning to his farm in Niafunké in northern Mali. Since then, however, he has also released a string of albums on the World Circuit label. Though he insists it's purely the result of working in an older version of the same tradition, he can sound astonishingly like Hooker. On "Roucky", on *The Source*, for example, it's hard to believe that the deep, resonant, authoritative guitar isn't coming from Hooker himself.

The Grammy-winning **Talking Timbuktu**, however, revealed the full breadth of Toure's music, playing in several distinct styles and singing in four of his eleven languages. It's Toure's album throughout, despite involving the collaboration of both African and American musicians, with Toure's own multi-instrumental prowess being superbly complemented – like so many artists in this book – by the slide guitar wizardry of Ry Cooder.

Two tracks, Sega and Banda, showcase Toure alone on the *njarka*, backed by his two omnipresent Malian percussionists. Most of the rest consists of extended improvisations, as the twin guitars of Toure and Cooder engagingly explore some simple, hypnotic riffs. For blues fans, the highlights of *Talking Timbuktu* have to be the two cuts that feature Clarence "Gatemouth" Brown. Ai Du, in particular, on which Brown contributes a viola part very much in keeping with Toure's previous *njarka* solos, is an irresistible, languorous groove.

Unless the dream pairing of Ali Farka Toure and John Lee Hooker playing together ever comes about, it's hard to imagine a more enjoyable fusion of African music and the blues than *Talking Timbuktu*, an album that proves the continuing vibrancy of the traditions from which it draws.

➲ We almost chose **The Source**, World Circuit, 1992

85

Big Joe Turner

Greatest Hits

Atlantic Jazz, 1989; recorded 1951–58

Joe Turner, the "Boss of the Blues", spent more than fifty years in the entertainment business. While he took his music seriously, his priority was always to please the crowds, not to embark on sensitive explorations of his own emotions. The greatest of the "blues shouters" started out before amplification had been invented, belting out songs loud enough not only to dominate whichever packed nightclub he was performing in, but to lure in passers-by for blocks around. When the microphone came along, he simply embraced it as an opportunity to yell even louder.

Although he straddled several genres – performing with the greats of jazz, boogie-woogie and swing, and having a seminal impact on the birth of rock'n'roll – Joe Turner was always based in the blues. He was already singing in the clubs of his native Kansas City, Missouri, long before his 21st birthday in 1932. At first he worked as a barman, breaking into song – cued by the boogie-woogie piano of Pete Johnson – as he prepared drinks. In 1938, the two men were recruited by John Hammond to appear in the first of his legendary "Spirituals to Swing" concerts in New York, and they never looked back. Within days, they recorded the classic "Roll 'Em Pete", and within two weeks they were opening the city's new Cafe Society club. Backed by no fewer than three pianists at once – Johnson, Albert Ammons and Meade Lux Lewis – Turner ignited the boogie-woogie craze that swept the nation.

After spending the war years recording in New York, Joe moved to California, where he worked for the National and Aladdin labels among many others. At the start of 1951, however, as he approached 40, his career seemed to be tailing off. Instead, thanks to a serendipitous linkup with Atlantic Records, he embarked on his most successful period. Atlantic's 21-track **Greatest Hits** compilation tells the unlikely story of how Turner became the most prominent member of that rare breed – traditional blues singers who actually increased their sales in the rock'n'roll era.

As far as Big Joe was concerned, they might have called his 1950s output rock'n'roll, but "it wasn't but a different name for the same music I been singing all my life." That's certainly true of the first few numbers here. The Chill Is On ("I've been your dog, ever since I've been your man"), Sweet Sixteen, as later recorded by B.B. King, and his first big smash, Chains Of Love, were all loud, conventional blues. It was Shake, Rattle And Roll, which topped the R&B charts in 1954, that changed everything. Though the song didn't make the pop charts until Bill Haley toned down its salacious lyrics – take the line about "a one-eyed cat peepin' in a seafood store" – Joe's version defined the exuberant, finger-popping sound of rock'n'roll. On the same day, he also recorded the even more raucous Well All Right, the template for many a subsequent Little Richard rocker.

"Shake, Rattle And Roll" inspired a stream of similar but enjoyable remakes, like Flip Flop And Fly and Leiber and Stoller's The Chicken And The Hawk. Turner didn't last long as a pop star – neither he nor Atlantic showed much interest in tailoring his material to suit the teen market – but on the other hand his sexual references and boastful persona struck a resonant chord with adult audiences. Thanks to such classic moments as the swinging standard Corrine Corrina, the gorgeous upbeat Blues In The Night, the call-and-response Crawdad Hole, and Honey Hush, with its exhilarating sax solo, Big Joe remained in demand, live and on record, until his death in 1985.

➲ We almost chose **Boss Of The Blues**, Atlantic, 1998

86

T-Bone Walker

T-Bone Blues

Catfish, 2000; recorded 1940–47

For anyone aware that T-Bone Walker is universally hailed as "the inventor of the electric guitar blues", and of his reputation as a consummate showman who inspired both Elvis and Jimi Hendrix, listening to his music for the first time may come as a real surprise. What leaps out at you is its sheer urbane sophistication: far from being crude or raucous, it's a smooth, mellow and heavily jazz–influenced sound. That the young T-Bone started out holding Blind Lemon Jefferson's tin cup on the streets of Texas only serves to emphasize how far and how fast he travelled in bringing the blues into the modern era. Catfish's 25-track compilation, **T-Bone Blues**, documents the crucial 1940s recordings in which he did it (and should not be confused with the equally powerful Atlantic album of the same name, which collects his 1950s work).

T-Bone Walker was never a trombonist – Aaron Thibeaux Walker's nickname derived from his middle name. Born in Linden, Texas, in 1910, he was raised in Dallas. As early as 1929, he recorded acoustic country blues as "Oak Cliff T-Bone". During the 1930s, he accompanied Ma Rainey and Ida Cox, played banjo with Cab Calloway, fell in with assorted big bands, and got his first steady gig in California as a tap-dancer. He was also initiated into playing electric guitar by Chuck Richardson in Oklahoma City; his friend and fellow pupil, Charlie Christian, is credited with pioneering the electric guitar in jazz.

It was as a singer that Walker returned to the studio, performing

T-Bone Blues in front of Les Hite and his Orchestra in New York in 1940 – the occasional guitar chord audible on the track was the work of Frank Pasley. Shortly thereafter, Walker and Hite parted company, and Walker devoted himself to exploring the potential of the latest technology. All the rest of the tracks on *T-Bone Blues* were recorded in California. Maddeningly, they don't appear here in chronological order, but the sleeve notes are detailed enough to piece the story together.

The new T-Bone sound was unveiled on a short session cut for Capitol in 1942. **I Got A Break Baby** opens with a mellifluous cascade of individual notes, which gather urgency as the first verse approaches, then reappear to frame and caress each vocal line. **Mean Old World** starts with a more extended instrumental passage, the guitar weaving in and out of Freddie Slack's boogie piano with sumptuous ease. Walker was not one of the great singers, but he oozed cool, marrying the intensity of the blues to the seductiveness of swing. Technically, the influence of Blind Lemon Jefferson remains evident in his single-string phrasing, but transposed to this hip, contemporary setting the blues sounded utterly reborn.

T-Bone really got into his stride in 1947, establishing the first of his many "small big bands". On-stage antics like playing the guitar between his legs, or behind his head while doing the splits, drove audiences wild, but it was his recording of **Call It Stormy Monday** that changed everything. B.B. King rushed out and bought an electric guitar as soon as he heard it, and T-Bone presented one of his own to John Lee Hooker in person.

Other tracks from that miraculous year – like the jazzy **Description Blues**, with its flamboyant runs and changes of pace; **T-Bone Shuffle**, which gave the world the "Texas shuffle"; and the blistering **T-Bone Jumps Again** – share that same electrifying sense of discovery. Walker continued to record seminal material throughout the 1950s, and was still releasing albums when he died in 1975, but this is where it all began – for him, and for everyone else.

➔ We almost chose **T-Bone Blues**, Atlantic, 1989

87

Muddy Waters

The Complete Plantation Recordings

Chess, 1993; recorded 1941–42

This CD is almost too good to be true. An hour's worth of Muddy Waters – arguably the greatest performer in blues history – recorded in the early 1940s as an unknown, barefoot sharecropper on the porch of his Mississippi cabin. The father of Chicago electric blues stands revealed as a master of rural acoustic blues; he even performs the self-same songs that formed his epoch-making first Chess single later that decade. Not that this CD is merely interesting: **The Complete Plantation Recordings** stand up in their own right. Only released in their entirety fifty years after they were made, they form a priceless, powerful statement of the Delta blues on the cusp of change.

By the time Library of Congress folklorist Alan Lomax came to Mississippi in August 1941, McKinley Morganfield was, in the words of his song, a full-grown man. Born April 4, 1915, in Rolling Fork, Mississippi, he had moved at the age of 3, to live with his grandmother on Stovall's Plantation outside Clarksdale after his mother's death. His grandmother nicknamed him "Muddy" for playing in the nearby stream, and "Waters" was added by neighbors. At 26, Muddy had been a full-time farm labourer for seventeen years and a musician every bit as long. Having started out on harp, he soon switched to guitar – according to some accounts, selling a mule in order to buy his first instrument. His earliest idol and mentor was Son House, and he was already playing with veteran violinist Henry "Son" Simms when Simms recorded alongside Charlie Patton in 1930.

Alan Lomax was primarily interested in finding songs rather than stars and arrived at Waters' cabin while trying to trace the origins of Robert Johnson's repertoire. Muddy's Country Blues drew heavily on Johnson's "Walkin' Blues" and revealed to Lomax that he was on the right track. However, as Muddy makes clear, in the fascinating interview fragments also included on the disc, Son House's own "My Black Mama" was the model for both songs. In any case, Waters certainly put his own stamp on the song: the assured dignity of his singing and bottleneck guitar work shines through in a rendition free of Johnson's customary angst.

The only other song originally released from that session, I Be's Troubled, is even more of a triumph. The prototype for "I Can't Be Satisfied" (see p.175), it's a more original and personal piece, and a perfect showcase for Waters' bottleneck prowess. Burr Clover Farm Blues, which follows, is a surprise, with Muddy singing the praises of his plantation boss, Howard Stovall, a pioneer of growing burr clover who had invented the first burr-clover harvester.

When Lomax returned in 1942, he was to record much more material. This includes four songs with Muddy as part of an acoustic group, the Son Simms Four, on which Simms' violin solos hark back to the sound of an earlier era. According to Muddy, they'd perform songs like "Home On The Range" when performing at local dances, but stuck close to the blues for Lomax's recordings. Take A Walk With Me, in particular, is strongly reminiscent of Johnson's "Sweet Home Chicago".

Muddy Waters' first session brought him neither fame nor acclaim. He was paid $20, plus two copies of the disc, which arrived with a letter reading: "I think that you should keep in practice because I feel sure that sometime you will get the break that you deserve." His true reward, however, was of inestimable value: "I really heard myself for the first time . . . I thought, man, this boy can sing the blues." Within a year of Lomax's second visit, armed with that self-belief, Waters was in Chicago.

➲ We almost chose **First Recording Sessions 1941–46**, Document, 1993

88

Muddy Waters

The Best Of Muddy Waters

Chess, 1987; recorded 1948–54

Without a decent compilation of Muddy Waters' fabulous Chess singles, there'd be a gaping hole in any blues collection. Which one to get is a thornier question. The latest matching pair of Chess re-issues, the two chronological volumes of *His Best*, can't really be faulted but the heart has to go for the LP that started it all – **The Best Of Muddy Waters**. As Waters' first album release, in the late 1950s, its impact was devastating. Waters had already enjoyed a string of R&B chart hits, but his sales weren't that big and he was in danger of getting left behind by rock'n'roll. Slowly but surely, this album found him a new, long-lasting and international audience and thereby helped to cement the blues as a permanent fixture on the world's musical landscape.

Received wisdom would have it that Muddy Waters arrived in Chicago in the mid-1940s and promptly invented an entirely new musical form. Looking back, over half a century later, a more gradual process can be discerned. Chess weren't (then) in the business of documenting history, so this LP kicks off with its culmination, I Just Want To Make Love To You. For sheer declamatory power, it's unbeatable, with Muddy's full-throated roar soaring above Otis Spann's authoritative piano and Little Walter's mournful, quasi-symphonic harp. Bassman Willie Dixon also wrote the song, with lyrics so uncompromising that they were still being censored in a TV advert in 1999.

Waters' first Chess single, I Can't Be Satisfied, appears here as the final track. It was recorded six years earlier, in 1948, which was in turn just six years after Alan Lomax's second trip to Mississippi. In the interim, Waters had joined the fifty thousand black Mississippians who migrated north to Chicago. There he swiftly hooked up with Big Bill Broonzy and set about adapting his music to the demands of the city. To some extent he saw amplification as a necessary evil more than an artistic stimulus. To survive as a musician he had to be heard, and to be heard in the clubs of Chicago he needed not only amplification but a full-scale band.

Though Muddy often avowed that he'd rather still be performing solo with his acoustic guitar, his great achievement was to work out how to deliver the true Delta blues in an urban setting. He became the greatest bandleader in the blues, to the extent that by his second decade with Chess he barely played guitar on his own records. At the outset, however, he was still playing slide guitar in a style that to his Chess producers seemed anachronistic rather than avant-garde. "I Can't Be Satisfied" is a reworking of "I Be's Troubled" from his Lomax recordings, kept ticking along at a faster tempo with the help of a solitary bass.

The huge local success of "Satisfied" encouraged Waters in his quest to give the blues a contemporary edge. Leonard Chess, the white owner of the label, had at first been dubious (and is often dismissed as having been motivated purely by money) but by the time he contributed his rudimentary drumming – or thumping, rather – to **Still A Fool** in 1951, he was firmly on board. He was duly supplanted by stellar sidemen like Little Walter, Jimmy Rogers on guitar and Fred Below on drums, but it was Willie Dixon's genius for putting the right words in the right mouth that completed the formula. Muddy was hardly sexually reticent but, with songs like **Hoochie Coochie Man** and **I'm Ready**, Dixon wrote him a succession of boastful epics that turned him into an icon. There were to be another thirty years of records every bit as accomplished, but for sheer impact these still deserve the title *The Best*.

➲ We almost chose **His Best 1947–55**, Chess, 1997

89

Muddy Waters

Muddy Waters At Newport

Chess, 1988; recorded 1960

While the 1950s studio recordings of Muddy Waters and his Chess stablemates remain the bedrock on which all subsequent electric blues has been based, it was **Muddy Waters at Newport** that did most to encourage musicians the world over to form their own bands and play the music themselves. The first and arguably the greatest live blues album captures the Muddy Waters band in its full glory at the very instant when the blues first began to win over a mass white audience.

Muddy Waters was booked to appear at 1960's Newport Jazz Festival after Nesuhi Ertegun of Atlantic Records saw him in a Chicago club. He was initially reluctant to take the gig, and it was pure luck that he played at all, on Sunday July 3. On the previous night, a crowd of ten thousand drunken teenagers had stormed the festival gates and been driven back with tear gas. It was too late to cancel Sunday afternoon's "educational" programme, designed to show the influence of the blues on jazz, but that evening's schedule, and the remaining two days, were abandoned.

That left Muddy's set as the climax of the festival. He was backed that day by Otis Spann on piano, James Cotton on harp, Pat Hare on guitar (in almost his last gig before being fired for drunkenness), Andrew Stevenson on bass and Francis Clay on drums. Honed to maximum power by nonstop gigging in Chicago, they were on devastating form, and the sedate white jazz aficionados were literally shaken out of their seats by their first exposure to full-on amplified blues.

Muddy kicked things off with some of his older crowd-pleasers: I Got My Brand On You, I'm Your Hoochie Coochie Man and Baby, Please Don't Go. At first he played slide guitar himself, though not the acoustic guitar he's pictured holding on the sleeve, which was John Lee Hooker's. As things warmed up, he left the guitar work to Hare, prowling the stage as he roared out Tiger In Your Tank. Forgetting the words, he blasted out the chorus over and over again; he may have lost the band along the way, but not the audience. Big Bill Broonzy's I Feel So Good kept up the pressure.

The real highlight is the awesome I've Got My Mojo Working, delivered with such stunning authority that he was instantly forced to repeat it as an encore. The frenzy of the crowd reached its peak at the end of James Cotton's harp solo, as Muddy took him in his arms and whirled him around the stage, while Francis Clay flailed ecstatically on the drums. Released as a single, the performance earned Muddy his first Grammy nomination.

The final number, Goodbye Newport Blues, was improvised on the spot around words written that afternoon by the celebrated black poet Langston Hughes, under the impression that there would never be another Newport Festival. It was sung by Otis Spann for the simple reason that Muddy couldn't read well enough to sing unfamiliar lyrics. The sensitivity of Spann's spur-of-the-moment piano accompaniment speaks volumes as to his importance in shaping the sound of the band.

At Newport marks a pivotal moment in Muddy Waters' career, as blues ceased to be the dance music of choice for urban blacks only to be seized upon by reverent whites. John Lee Hooker made his first festival appearance that same day and both men were seminal influences on the countless rock bands who soon sprang up on both sides of the Atlantic. *At Newport* is the monument to Muddy as he'd love to be remembered – in his prime as leader of the finest live band on the planet.

⮕ We almost chose **Hard Again**, Blue Sky, 1987

90

Junior Wells

Hoodoo Man Blues

Delmark, 1990; recorded 1965

Even if **Hoodoo Man Blues** wasn't any good, it would mark a milestone in blues history. It wasn't just Junior Wells' first album, it was the first album as such to be cut by any Chicago bluesman. Full-length compilations of previously released singles were already on the market, but prior to Wells no one had entered the studio specifically in order to record an entire album. Remarkably, however, *Hoodoo Man Blues* stands as not only the first, but also one of the very best, capturing all the energy and excitement of a pride of young Chicago lions as they scented their first kill.

Despite being only 30 in 1965, Junior Wells was already a twenty-year veteran of the Chicago scene. Having first learned to play the harmonica from his Memphis neighbour, "Little Junior" Parker, he'd moved north with his mother in 1946. There, at the age of 12, he had the nerve to sit in with Muddy Waters during a club gig, while Waters' harpist Little Walter was taking a break. Walter, who was himself just 17, was impressed enough to take Wells under his wing. Muddy went further, and informally "adopted" the boy, signing court papers to keep him out of jail for juvenile violence. Wells was soon recording under his own name, and also starring as one of the Aces. In 1952, a surprisingly amicable swap saw Little Walter launching his own solo career with the Aces, while Wells took over his spot with Muddy.

After a troubled stint in the army, Wells spent the next ten years cutting singles for assorted minor labels. Though he first teamed up with the young Buddy Guy in 1958, the "Chicago Blues Band" featured on *Hoodoo Man Blues*, which added Jack Myers on bass and Billy Warren on drums, was put together for the occasion by Delmark boss, Bob Koester. The album took just eight hours to record, and aimed to reproduce the dynamics and structure of a typical live set. Its opening track, the funky **Snatch It Back And Hold It**, makes it very clear that this is the *contemporary* blues, with Wells "hey hey"-ing like James Brown even as he announces that "I ain't got no brand new bag."

Buddy Guy was by now Chicago's hottest session guitarist, and Chess, who owned his contract, only allowed him to be billed as "Friendly Chap" on the original release. At his least flamboyant and most sensitive, his contribution is judged to perfection throughout. It's Junior Wells' show, nonetheless: his harp handles virtually all the solos, and is especially atmospheric on slower numbers such as the extraordinary **In The Wee Hours** and the extended workout **Early In The Morning**. The band also do justice to chestnuts like **Yonder Wall** and **Hound Dog**, and swing out over two takes of the Latin-flavoured instrumental **Chitlin Con Carne**.

Wells' greatest hero was Sonny Boy Williamson I, and the two Williamson numbers here gave him the chance to honour his master's memory in the best possible way. **Good Morning School Girl** has a relentless, driving authority, while **Hoodoo Man Blues**, with its memorable refrain of "somebody done hoodooed the hoodoo man", had already become, along with "Messin' With The Kid", one of Wells' two lifelong signature tunes. His voice worked best on that kind of swaggering, declamatory material; elsewhere, his singing can be the one weak link in the chain.

Junior Wells continued to perform and record, both solo and in partnership with Buddy Guy, right up to his death in 1998. He never again quite sounded as if he had anything to prove; but then, after *Hoodoo Man Blues*, that's hardly surprising.

➲ We almost chose **The Best Of The Vanguard Years**, Vanguard, 1998

91

Peetie Wheatstraw

The Devil's Son-In-Law

Story of Blues; recorded 1930–41

Best-selling 1930s pianist William Bunch adopted the name "Peetie Wheatstraw" from an obscure figure of Southern folklore. That Bunch also styled himself as "the Devil's son-in-law" and the "High Sherriff from Hell" suggests that "Peetie" too was of dubious character, but no one now remembers who he was or what he's supposed to have done. Similarly, for all his celebrity among his contemporaries, Bunch/Wheatstraw himself has now faded from memory. **The Devil's Son-in-Law** gives modern listeners a cut-price opportunity to rediscover him with tracks drawn from every period of his career.

Wheatstraw was unusual in being equally proficient at both piano and guitar, which in his case meant not very good at either. More significantly, he was one of the first blues musicians to trade explicitly on a bad-man persona. He cultivated the image of the heavy-drinking, hard-loving, fist-fighting bluesman throughout his career, winning over his audiences with his insouciant drawl of a voice as much as with his hard-bitten lyrics. He could even be claimed as the first "gangster" artist: his references to bootlegging, kidnapping and general gunslinging, in songs such as Gangster's Blues, made him one of the few black musicians active in 1930s Chicago to refer to the city's best-known business.

The future Peetie Wheatstraw was born in Ripley, Tennessee, in 1902. Until he moved to East St Louis in 1929, he regarded himself as a guitarist, so he'd only been a professional pianist for a year when he made his debut for Vocalion in 1930. That would explain why Don't Feel Welcome Blues sounds so much like a conventional guitar-based blues of the period. As he warns his baby, "don't ever turn a stranger from your door, he may be your best friend, you will never know", Wheatstraw's vocal delivery, complete with high-pitched hums, is uncannily like that later heard from Robert Johnson, among others.

By 1934, when he recorded These Times, the Peetie Wheatstraw persona had become fixed in the popular imagination through songs like "Devil's Son-in-Law" and "Pete Wheatstraw", neither of which is included here. So, too, had the Wheatstraw trademark of singing "ooh, well, well" in the third line of virtually every verse in every song: it sounds utterly familiar these days, of course, but someone had to think of it first.

Despite his guitar-toting sleeve photograph, Wheatstraw doesn't play guitar on this CD. For the rest of the 1930s, however, he was always accompanied by a guitarist, and often a very good one. On More Good Whiskey Blues from 1935, a reaction to the end of Prohibition and of the "bad whiskey" that went with it, it's Casey Bill Weldon. Kokomo Arnold plays inventive high fills on Meat Cutter Blues, Fairasee Woman and the entertaining Crazy With The Blues, while Lonnie Johnson is gloriously jaunty and fluent on What More Can A Man Do? and the saucy I Want Some Sea Food.

From 1939 onwards, Wheatstraw didn't even play piano on his records, either. No one knows why; it may just have been because they sounded better without him. The last few tracks here show him in a lively small-band setting, with Lil Armstrong on piano and Jonah Jones on trumpet on "Gangster's Blues", and Champion Jack Dupree at the keyboard on Hearse Man Blues and Bring Me Flowers While I'm Living. These last two, recorded in November 1941, proved prophetic: Wheatstraw was killed a few weeks later when his car hit a train. With his gift for self-promotion, the final line of his final song provided his epitaph: "If I don't go to heaven, ooh, well, well, I sure don't need no flowers in hell."

➲ We almost chose **The Last Straw**, Catfish, 1999

92

Bukka White

The Complete Bukka White

Columbia, 1994; recorded 1937 and 1940

Contrary to the title, Columbia's **Complete Bukka White** reissue does not represent Bukka's entire output. However, these fourteen sides, recorded for Vocalion in Chicago in 1937 and 1940, give a complete picture of one of the blues' finest guitarists and songwriters at the peak of his powers. Their most striking feature – their sense of passionate urgency – is due to the fact that the first two sides were cut as White awaited trial for shooting a man during a juke-house brawl, while the remaining twelve were recorded as soon as he was released from his two-year incarceration for assault in Mississippi's Parchman Farm jail. These latter, made at the tail end of the fashion for acoustic blues (when swing music was becoming ever more popular) are generally regarded as constituting the last great country blues session ever recorded.

Named after the nineteenth-century black educator, Booker T. Washington, White became known as "Bukka" thanks to a record-company error. Born in the Mississippi hill country, ninety miles east of Clarksdale, on November 12, 1909, by the age of 10 he had moved to the Delta to work on his uncle's farm. Although he never met the veteran singer, he later recalled how "I always wanted to be like old Charlie Patton." His chance to emulate his hero came in 1930, when he made his first recordings in Memphis. Only three of these were released: two gospel sides, on which Bukka was billed as "The Singing Preacher", and the frenetic The Panama Limited, a train song on which the percussive guitar playing that supported his vocal impersonations sounded fit to break the instrument in two.

That same kind of heavily accented strumming on an open-G-tuned steel National guitar made White's 1937 recording of **Shake 'Em On Down** a significant regional hit. The technique remains associated with the hill country this day, as evidenced by R.L. Burnside's 1994 cover version on *Too Bad Jim*. Even more than his slide guitar prowess, however, it was White's songs that earned him lasting fame. Though White was a former boxer, imprisoned for violence and imposing enough to be known by his fellow inmates as "Barrelhouse", these songs display not only a deeply personal introspection but also a rare degree of tenderness. Their intensity is somehow reinforced by their lack of verbal dexterity; in some, every line ends with an almost identical rhyme, and most simply reiterate rather than develop their basic theme.

White's tour de force, **Fixin' To Die Blues**, is one of the absolute classics of country blues, in which he mourns his imminent death – "I know I was born to die, but I hate to leave my children cryin'" – while recalling the domestic joys he's about to lose – "so many nights by the fireside." The similarly poignant **Strange Place Blues** finds him standing on his mother's grave, lamenting that "I wish I could find someone to take her place."

For the 1940 sessions, White was paid $17.50 per side, while Washboard Sam got another $20 for his, at times, demented attempts to keep up with Bukka's ferocious strumming. In later life, White lived in Memphis, where he played electric rhythm guitar in Beale Street blues bands at the time his younger cousin, B.B. King, was making his mark. During the 1960s, he was "re-discovered" by West Coast blues enthusiasts, who located him by the simple expedient of mailing a general-delivery letter addressed to "Bukka White, Old Blues Singer, Aberdeen, Mississippi." For the remaining years before his death in February 1977, he toured the international festival circuit and made a number of unfocused but nonetheless interesting albums.

⊃ We almost chose **Sky Songs**, Arhoolie, 1991

93

Sonny Boy Williamson I

Shake The Boogie

Blue Boar Records, 1999; recorded 1937–47

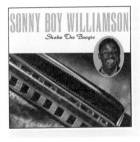

Imitation may be the sincerest form of flattery, but harmonica giant John Lee "Sonny Boy" Williamson could be forgiven for resenting the usurper who stole his name and sabotaged his reputation. Williamson, a stalwart of the Chicago-based Bluebird label, deserves to be considered as the first great trailblazer in modern blues harp; instead, he's doomed to be remembered as merely the first Sonny Boy Williamson. That's to distinguish him from Sonny Boy Williamson II, who arrived in town a couple of years later to begin an even more successful recording career. While the second Sonny Boy was undeniably a major artist, you only have to listen to the first to realize just how much he owed to his predecessor.

Sonny Boy's seminal Bluebird sides are now available on any number of CD compilations, not all of which make it clear which Sonny Boy they're dealing with. Blue Boar's **Shake The Boogie** is chosen here on grounds of its low price, comprehensive 25-track selection and informative sleeve notes.

Born in Jackson, Tennessee, in 1914, Williamson learned to play the harp in Memphis during the late 1920s. At that time, in the hands of exponents like Noah Lewis and Hammie Nixon, the harmonica was just beginning to supplant the fiddle in the line-up of blues ensembles. Williamson's achievement, on reaching Chicago in the mid-1930s, was to propel the harp to the forefront. Although he never entirely abandoned the traditional subordinate role of playing background chords, as leader of his own band he was able to indulge in intricate single-note melodies that dominated the overall sound. A pioneer of the "cross-harp" or "second position" technique, in which a harp tuned to the key of C is played in G to make it easier to "bend" notes, he also used the harmonica to deliver seamless responses to his own vocal phrasings.

In following Sonny Boy's recordings in sequence, *Shake The Boogie* succinctly demonstrates the differences between prewar and postwar Chicago blues. Williamson's debut performances, on which he's backed by either two guitars or guitar and mandolin, remain clearly rooted in the repertoire and arrangements he'd brought from the rural South. Year by year, more beef was added to the backing, with the addition of piano, drums, bass and electric guitar, but those early sides remain sensational – not least because of the songs themselves. Williamson's very first session, with Big Joe Williams and Robert Nighthawk in May 1937, produced classics of the order of **Good Morning School Girl**, **Bluebird Blues** and **Sugar Mama Blues**. His hard-edged harp stylings stood out even more a year later, when he blasted out **Decoration Blues** and **Sunnyland** against the fluttering mandolin accompaniment of old buddy Yank Rachell.

From 1939 onwards, pianists such as Walter Davis, Joshua Altheimer and Eddie Boyd helped Williamson shape the fundamental sound of urban Chicago blues. Numbers like **Miss Ida Lee**, **My Little Machine** and **Ground Hog Blues** have been staples ever since. Tragically, the spell in 1943 when Muddy Waters worked as Williamson's guitarist coincided with the wartime ban on recording. After the war, Sonny Boy picked up where he'd left off, working with Big Bill Broonzy and the young Willie Dixon on swing- and boogie-influenced material like **Shake The Boogie**, **Mellow Chick Swing** and **Bring Another Half Pint**. Had he not been stabbed outside a nightclub, at the age of just 34, he might have continued to overshadow disciples such as Little Walter and his own namesake; as it is, these epic Bluebird recordings are all that remain.

➲ We almost chose **The Bluebird Recordings 1937–38**, RCA, 1996

94

Sonny Boy Williamson II

King Biscuit Time

Arhoolie, 1989; recorded 1951–65

Although Alec "Rice" Miller was – by at least fifteen years – the older of the two harp players who styled themselves Sonny Boy Williamson, by all accounts save his own he was the second claimant to the name. The first was John Lee Williamson, who recorded for the Bluebird label in the late 1930s (see p.185). The second, who was also known as Alex Ford, or Willie Williams, was born in 1897, or 1908 – or maybe 1909. When he died, in 1965, he was buried in Tutwiler, Mississippi, so it makes sense to assume that he was born somewhere nearby.

Whoever he was, this Sonny Boy Williamson has a strong claim to be regarded as the originator of amplified blues harp. He may not quite rival Little Walter as its greatest exponent, but his rough-hewn genius, combined with his extraordinary way with words – both writing them and singing them – and the force of his personality, make his records even more compelling. The hour-long **King Biscuit Time** anthology includes not only his first studio efforts, made for Trumpet Records in Jackson Mississippi in 1951, but also his last ever session within days of his death. A perfect complement to his equally irresistible Chess outings (see p.189), it shows a mature, confident artist who was nonetheless still experimenting as he searched for the formula that would bring him overdue recognition and rewards.

"Rice" Miller was already an itinerant musician by 1930. Even discounting his own tall tales, he seems to have played with

Robert Johnson and was married for a while to Howlin' Wolf's sister. His big break came in 1941 when, together with Robert Junior Lockwood, Johnson's adopted son, he started appearing on the daily *King Biscuit Time* radio show, out of Helena, Arkansas. He began to call himself Sonny Boy Williamson, and the show's sponsors cashed in by marketing a new line of Sonny Boy Corn Meal complete with his caricature. Among the eager listeners being exposed to electric guitar and amplified harmonica for the first time was Muddy Waters, just across the Mississippi.

It was another ten years before Lillian McMurry invited Sonny Boy to record for her new Trumpet label. He seized the opportunity to lay down two half-extemporized, deeply personal songs: Eyesight To The Blind and Cross My Heart. Their success meant he was soon back in the studio, this time backed by the fluid guitar of Elmore James. In a single day they cut eight more songs, bursting with such Williamson trademarks as the bawdy, fierce eroticism of She Brought Life Back To The Dead and the bitter recrimination of Nine Below Zero. They even found time for Elmore James to make his first and finest recording of Dust My Broom, included here on account of Sonny Boy's harp contribution.

Williamson delivered six more tracks in December 1951, including Mr Down Child, an unrecorded Robert Johnson song learned by Lockwood from the man himself (while incapacitated by diarrhoea). The classic here, however, was the impassioned Mighty Long Time, in which Williamson's doom-laden harp was supported only by a solitary vocal bass-line, as he mourned having been abandoned for so long that the carpet had faded on the floor.

As a final bonus, the CD adds on a complete thirteen-minute edition of the *King Biscuit Show* from May 1965, the month Williamson died. Backed by a gloriously ramshackle band, he belts out such unlikely requests as Stormy Monday, and plugs his gig that night in Greenwood, Mississippi.

➲ We almost chose **Goin' In Your Direction**, Trumpet, 1994

95

Sonny Boy Williamson II

Down And Out Blues

Chess, 1988; recorded 1955–58

The last of the veteran Deep South bluesmen to triumph for Chess, Sonny Boy Williamson II delayed his move to the label until the last possible moment. Even then it came about by chance. The fact that Mississippi's Trumpet Records had the decency to give its artists proper contracts meant that when the label failed in late 1954 Sonny Boy ended up being traded to Chess. But when he finally arrived he landed on his feet. Furnished with the entire Muddy Waters band – including Muddy himself – as his sidemen, he unleashed a string of superb, assured singles that built him an enduring reputation even as the devastating onslaught of rock'n'roll was unleashed. Willie Dixon in particular provided his songs with a much tighter feel and structure, while allowing Sonny Boy's character to remain centre stage.

To call Sonny Boy Williamson a "complicated" man is probably overgenerous – those who knew him in the Delta were more likely to describe him as "real evil". Tales of vicious knife fights with fellow musicians (specifically, his great rival Little Walter) are all too credible. And yet somehow his sly, knowing vocal style, delivering even the most intricate of lyrics with the comic timing of a master, is utterly seductive. Witness too his cartoon-like transformation on being taken up by the British "beat" musicians of the 1960s, sporting a tailored two-tone suit, plus crisp shirt and tie, and rounding things off with a bowler hat. Film from the period reveals him as a charismatic showman, playing his harp hands-free, chewing on it like a cigar and even taking it entirely into his mouth, driving the music forward even as he distanced himself from his audience with a wicked leer.

The very first moment of **Down And Out Blues** finds Sonny Boy in mid-conversation: "Well I'm going down the road, stopping Fanny Mae, gonna tell Fanny what I heard her boyfriend say." Don't Start Me To Talkin' is a saga of small-town gossip and intrigue; back home in Helena, Arkansas, they can still point out the landmarks he mentions. For follow-up I Don't Know onwards, Muddy Waters was replaced on guitar by Williamson's old stomping partner Robert Lockwood Junior, but the band remained intact. Adorned with an even more exaggerated stop-motion lurch, it opens in a similar vein: "At 11.45, the phone began to ring." As Sonny Boy half-talks, half-sings us through a crisis in his relationship, his voice remains sardonic, his emotions expressed instead through his wailing harp.

So many of these songs share a palpable, ominous tension. Even as he avows on All My Love In Vain that "a woman is the glory of a man", murder is clearly on his mind, while the relentless vamp of The Key bristles with implicit threat. The menace of Your Funeral And My Trial, in which he begs his baby to "cut out that off-the-wall jive", could hardly be plainer. The atmosphere is easier to take on more playful material like 1957's Fattening Frogs For Snakes, the endless verses of which Sonny Boy relishes with all the sassy confidence of Chuck Berry, and 1958's Wake Up Baby, the slapstick folk standard whose variants include the Dubliners' "Seven Drunken Nights".

Sonny Boy Williamson continued to record for Chess for another five years after *Down And Out Blues*. Thanks to Willie Dixon's "American Folk Blues Festival" tours, he then enjoyed a final swansong of acclaim and riches in Europe, where he was lionized by young turks like the Yardbirds and the Animals. He returned to Arkansas for the last time in 1965, and died shortly afterwards.

➲ We almost chose **His Best**, Chess, 1997

96

Various Artists

Before The Blues Vol.1

Yazoo, 1996; recorded 1927–32

Yazoo's three-volume **Before The Blues** series does not literally document recordings made before the emergence of the blues. It couldn't, since the blues as a distinct genre came into being at the same time as the recording industry. Some would say that the blues took shape *because* of the new commercial possibilities, as artists who had previously played a wide range of material limited their musical horizons in order to cash in on the current craze. *Before The Blues* reflects the early days before definitions became too rigid, as folk artists across America exhausted their repertoires in the hope of appealing to record buyers. Many of the performers on this disc have been acclaimed as pioneers of the blues, but at this stage most were doing no more than tagging the word "blues" onto the names of time-honoured traditional pieces.

Ultimately, *Before The Blues* is an excuse for an enjoyable trawl through the Yazoo archives, which turns up a delicious assortment of beautiful ballads, ragtime romps, sacred sermons, jug-band jives and country-flavoured instrumentals. In his fascinating sleeve notes, Richard Nevins uses this eclectic mix to point out that even up to the end of the nineteenth century there was little distinction between black and white music in the southern United States. Eschewing simplistic notions of the blues as the black American transmission of the African heritage, he shows that many "blues standards" drew instead on centuries-old European ballads or popular vaudeville tunes. Thus Dick Devall's Tom Sherman's Room, a version of the Scottish ballad also known as "Streets Of Laredo", later became Blind Willie McTell's "Dying Crapshooter's Blues". The seeds of another classic, Blind Lemon Jefferson's "See That My Grave Is Kept Clean", can be seen in the guitar and mandolin duet of Joe Evans and Arthur McClain, on Two White Horses In A Line. The "two white horses standing on the burying ground" re-appear on Papa Harvey Hull's France Blues.

One way in which rural black and white music diverged during the twentieth century was in instrumentation; while country musicians stuck with fiddle and banjo, bluesmen switched to pianos and guitars. Dance pieces recorded before then now seem impossible to place as either black or white, blues or country. For what it's worth, Forked Deer, by Taylor's Kentucky Boys, was both, with black fiddler Jim Booker playing alongside white banjoist Marion Underwood. The Mississippi Mud Steppers, whose Jackson Stomp was intended for white audiences, were black; one member was the ubiquitous Armenter Chatmon, who later recorded as Bo Carter. Virtuoso banjoist Buell Kazee, whose stunning John Hardy was reprised in 1998 by Alvin Youngblood Hart, was white; and, as for the equally accomplished Bayless Rose, whose banjo instrumental Jamestown Exhibition reminded Samuel Charters of the African kora, no one knows.

Of the tracks by artists later identified with the blues, standouts include Mississippi John Hurt's Stack O'Lee Blues, Robert Wilkins' I'll Go With Her Blues and Henry Thomas' square-dance Run Mollie Run, with its echoes of "Li'l Liza Jane". There are also a couple of lovely numbers by men who remain barely known because they recorded so little. Blind guitarist Willie Walker contributes some delightful Carolinan finger-picking on Dupree Blues, a ballad by a white Atlanta newspaper seller about a true-life murder in 1922 that has since become a staple as "Betty And Dupree". Finally, Bye Bye Baby Blues, by Texan guitarist Little Hat Jones, is so gorgeous it's almost worth buying the entire CD for that alone.

⮑ We almost chose **Before The Blues Vol.2**, Yazoo, 1996

97

Various Artists

The Chess Blues-Rock Songbook

Chess, 1998; recorded 1950–67

If you could only take one blues CD to the proverbial desert island, it would have to be a "best of Chess" compilation. The problem is that there's just too much great stuff to squeeze onto any one anthology. Anyone who loves the blues needs at the very least a full disc each of Muddy Waters, Howlin' Wolf and Sonny Boy Williamson, which leaves no room for any of their staggering array of labelmates. However, choosing to include the budget-priced twin-CD **Chess Blues-Rock Songbook** here serves a treble purpose.

First of all it features a representative selection of the true giants. Thus Muddy gets four tracks, including I'm Your Hoochie Coochie Man and I Just Want To Make Love To You; Wolf has four as well, including Spoonful and Back Door Man; and Sonny Boy I appears twice, with Bring It On Home and Help Me. Second, there's a handful of one-off classics by bona fide blues artists who otherwise didn't manage to squeeze into these pages, as with Jimmy Rogers' Walking By Myself, Lowell Fulson's Reconsider Baby and Eddie Boyd's 24 Hours. And finally, a dozen or so of the 36 tracks pay tribute to Chess' significance in early rock'n'roll. Although both Bo Diddley and Chuck Berry started out as bluesmen, neither remained sufficiently close to the blues to have an album included in this book. Hearing tracks like Bo's I'm A Man and Chuck's Roll Over Beethoven in this context, however, serves as a powerful reminder of their roots.

You don't have to subscribe to the rationale behind *The Chess*

Blues-Rock Songbook in order to enjoy listening to it. All these songs have indeed entered the repertoires of countless rock bands over the decades. However, this is wonderful music in its own right; it's not somehow validated because other people tried to copy it. The fact that Foghat and Gerry And The Pacemakers both covered **My Babe**, or that Freddie And The Dreamers and Judas Priest did the same for **Johnny B. Goode**, adds nothing to the achievements of Little Walter and Chuck Berry respectively.

The Chess label proper was founded in Chicago in 1950 by two brothers, Leonard and Phil Chess. They'd arrived from Poland with their parents in 1928 – the family name was actually Chez – and graduated from running music clubs to setting up Aristocat Records in 1947. At first, their interests were focused on jazz, but a surprise hit with Muddy Waters' "I Can't Be Satisfied" in 1948 persuaded Leonard to concentrate on blues instead. Quite how much credit he deserves for Chess' subsequent triumphs remains controversial; Muddy himself said both that Leonard was "the one person responsible for my success" and that "he didn't know nothing about no blues." Unarguably, the label's heyday ended with Leonard's sudden death in 1969.

There's only room here to run through the high-water marks of that glorious twenty-year span. Many early releases, such as Willie Mabon's **I Don't Know** and John Lee Hooker's **Sugar Mama**, were leased from other local labels, while scouting further afield came up with such gems as, from New Orleans, Sugar Boy Crawford's **Jock-A-Mo** (better known as "Iko Iko"), and **See You Later Alligator** by white teenager Bobby Charles. The characteristic Chess sound only came to full fruition when the brothers opened their own studio in 1954. Willie Dixon's pivotal role as bandleader and songwriter is everywhere apparent: as well as nine hits for other artists, this set includes his own rare cut of **Wang Dang Doodle**. Even if, by the late 1960s, Chess was responding to trends rather than initiating them, Little Milton's **More And More** and Etta James' **Tell Mama** are fit to stand with the best soul of the period.

➲ We almost chose **Chess Blues Guitar 1949–1969**, Chess, 1998

98

Various Artists

I Can't Be Satisfied

Yazoo, 1997; recorded 1925–34

Even the subtitle of the Yazoo compilation **I Can't Be Satisfied** – "Early American Women Blues Singers, Volume 1" – does little to hint at the rare and unexpected treasures that lie within. The women featured here aren't the familiar "classic" blues singers of the 1920s, like Bessie Smith and Ma Rainey, who came to fame on the vaudeville circuit; instead they're their rural equivalent, much closer in spirit to the dirt-poor backwoods bluesmen of the Deep South, and frequently known through a solitary session cut somewhere on the road. The Depression put a stop to that kind of speculative recording of local musical traditions, so *I Can't Be Satisfied* now stands as an invaluable document.

Not that the eighteen women featured on this 23-track CD necessarily shared much more than their gender. Their recordings range across the full amazing spectrum of early twentieth-century black music. Thus Bessie Tucker's haunting Penitentiary is basically an old-style Texas "holler", on which she all but shouts over the minimal accompaniment, while Hattie Hudson's Black Hand Blues, a variant on "Alabama Bound", boasts a sophisticated piano arrangement and up-to-the-minute lyrics describing how "the flappers are doing all the mooching." Similarly, Lottie Kimbrough delivers a delightful melodic rendition of Rolling Log Blues atop a beautifully conceived guitar backing, whereas Elizabeth Johnson's vernacular Be My Kid Blues derives its haphazard charm from the stop-start contributions of a cornet and a pair of clomping wood blocks.

Perhaps the most unusual sound of all is heard on Lizzie Washington's My Low Down Brown, on which her low-register vocals are embellished by the tinklings of Lonnie Johnson's brother James on a celeste, and the loud breathing makes you feel as though you're in the room with them. A similar flavour of eaves-dropping on a bygone era permeates two tracks that feature the Memphis Jug Band: Hattie Hart's knowing duet with Will Shade on Papa's Got Your Bath Water On; and Jennie Clayton's appealingly tremulous State Of Tennessee Blues, from 1927.

At the head of the select band of rural female performers who played their own instruments stands Geeshie Wiley. Though she's remembered as having lived in Natchez, Mississippi, her unusual name, and her unique guitar framework for Eagles On A Half, suggest a connection with the Georgia Sea Islands. She often worked as a duo with another woman guitarist, Elvie Thomas, and their Pick Poor Robin Clean is the definitive rendition of a traditional allegory about oppression in the South. Memphis Minnie, whose career and reputation lasted far longer than Wiley's, adds the poignant Outdoor Blues. Another solo per-former, Mattie Delaney, who was recorded in Memphis at the age of 25 in 1930, clearly modelled her guitar playing on that of Charlie Patton and Tommy Johnson. On Down The Big Road Blues she adopted a similar persona, too: "my mother said six months before I was born, she was gonna have a girl-child wouldn't never stay at home."

Patton appears in person on two tracks recorded with Bertha Lee in 1934. Mind Reader Blues reflects the fact that their rocky four-year marriage was already over – "my man done so many wrong things 'til I had to leave the town" – while Yellow Bee is a reworking of Memphis Minnie's signature tune, "Bumble Bee". Blind Willie McTell plays guitar and sings behind his wife, Ruby Glaze, on Lonesome Day Blues, while Blind Blake backs Bertha Henderson on That Lonesome Rave, on which she sings of how "the grass is growing over the man I love."

⮕ We almost chose **Blue Ladies**, Memphis Archives, 1995

Various Artists

The Real Bahamas

Nonesuch Explorer, 1998; recorded 1965

On the face of it, the idea that the place to search for a "missing link" between American blues and the music of Africa might be in the Bahamas, halfway between the two continents, sounds too banal to be true. And in truth, the recordings on **The Real Bahamas**, collected on the islands in 1965 by two young musicologists, Peter Siegel and Jody Stecher, are not exactly the blues. For anyone interested in the origins of American popular music, however – let alone anyone who simply enjoys the interplay of human voices and acoustic guitar – they're utterly irresistible.

The reason for academic interest in Bahamian music is that it may represent the closest modern approximation to the sounds heard on the plantations of the American South during the early nineteenth century – the time and the place black American music emerged as a distinct form. The Bahamas were originally colonized at the same time as the Carolinas in 1670. However, in distinction to the mainland, the slaves imported there from Africa were not dispersed on arrival and were thus able to retain their tribal identities and traditions. With the American Revolution, those Carolina settlers loyal to the British throne retreated to the Bahamas, taking with them the popular songs and musical influences that had already infiltrated from Europe. Since then, the Bahamas have remained relatively undisturbed, and the music of its black population remains rooted in the distant past.

The actual sound of *The Real Bahamas* is an unalloyed delight: while achingly pure and fresh, it's very far from being simple.

When this material originally appeared – as two LPs released in 1966 and 1978 – it was heralded as a revelation. Without ever quite fitting into any familiar genre, it echoes and illuminates the American folk, blues and spiritual traditions in constantly stimulating ways.

Almost every song is religious, in what the compilers call the "rhyming spiritual" form. Most are a cappella, with their complex rhythms being created by having several different voices singing or chanting at different speeds at the same time. The words themselves are often barely relevant, with the same verbal fragments and refrains cropping up again and again. These are field recordings, made in the performers' houses, on back porches or even alleyways, and they're largely improvised. The effect is reminiscent of the early blues songsters and evangelists, with well-known songs and hymns being adapted and embroidered to suit individual tastes; thus the first track, We'll Understand It Better By And By, is a variation of Blind Willie Johnson's "Bye And Bye I'm Going To See The King". The group harmonies on Up In The Heaven Shouting and My Lord Help Me To Pray have to be heard to be believed.

What makes *The Real Bahamas* truly extraordinary, however, is that in hunting the vernacular the researchers captured a virtuoso – guitarist Joseph Spence. Cited by Dr John as the only musician on any instrument who shared Professor Longhair's idiosyncratic sense of rhythm, Spence subsequently became a recording and coffeehouse star in his own right. He appears on nine of the 28 tracks here – albeit sometimes only as a singer – and that's when the album truly comes alive.

Spence's two solo guitar pieces – Don't Take Everybody To Be Your Friend, on which his melodic playing recalls Son House, and the intricate Won't That Be A Happy Time – are the instrumental highlights. Best of all, however, is the exquisitely touching ensemble number with his family, I Bid You Goodnight, a wake song that was later covered by the Grateful Dead.

⮑ We almost chose **Joseph Spence: The Spring Of '65**, Rounder, 1992

Various Artists

The Roots Of Robert Johnson

Yazoo, 1990; recorded 1927–37

If you don't already share the blues world's near-universal reverence for Robert Johnson, the concept of a CD anthology of the music that influenced him may well leave you cold. However, there's more to Yazoo's **The Roots Of Robert Johnson** than just an eye-catching peg for another compilation of prewar blues, let alone a dry academic exercise. All its fourteen tracks are there for a good reason: some mark major stylistic innovations, others simply show some particular performer at the height of his or her powers.

If you *are* familiar with Johnson's work, on the other hand, the album comes with a built-in bonus – every track also sheds light on some aspect of the Johnson canon. The overall effect will almost certainly be to enhance your appreciation. True, it becomes clear that Johnson didn't conjure his art out of thin air – if he *did* meet the Devil at that Delta crossroads, Satan clearly gave him a phonograph and a stack of records. He worked within a tradition, and *The Roots Of Robert Johnson* celebrates the strength and richness of that tradition.

Any claim for Johnson to be regarded as an original songwriter would swiftly be dismissed by a jury given this CD as Exhibit A. But even if he gathered each of his ingredients from some other source, Johnson's achievement was to blend them into his own glorious amalgam. At the most basic of levels, no one aware of the blues as an oral medium should be surprised to find that Johnson appropriated phrases, couplets and verses from previously recorded material. Thus, Leroy Carr's 1935 refrain of "it's hard to tell, it's hard to tell" on When The Sun Goes Down obviously presages Johnson's "Love In Vain" from two years later, while Johnson echoed Scrapper Blackwell's "Baby don't you want to go" (from 1934's Kokomo Blues) on his own "Sweet Home Chicago" in 1936.

The parallels go much deeper than that, of course. Several entire songs here, such as Skip James' 1931 22–20 Blues and Son House's 1930 Preachin' The Blues, were all but unchanged in Johnson's hands (in these examples, as "32–20 Blues" and "Preaching Blues" respectively). In other instances, he set different, but still not necessarily original, words to the same tunes, as when he turned the Mississippi Sheiks' Sitting On Top Of The World into "Come On In My Kitchen".

Stephen Calt's illuminating sleeve notes highlight many fascinating, but less immediately obvious, aspects of the performances. Stressing that Johnson's major contribution to the blues guitar was to master the technique of playing a constant "boogie bass" while still maintaining the standard voice–guitar dialogue on the upper strings, he pays tribute to Charlie Patton's Revenue Man Blues (from 1934) as having pointed the way forward. Johnnie Temple's 1935 Lead Pencil Blues is an even more striking example: Temple may well have learned the boogie from Johnson himself, and stresses it here enough to sound to modern ears like Status Quo. Also known as "walking bass", this style was clearly derived from piano bass-lines, which is why the piano tracks here from Skip James and Leroy Carr don't seem at all out of place.

That Son House is represented by both "Preachin' The Blues" and My Black Mama underlines the strength of his repertoire, but also makes clear how much it gained from being slowed down and more skilfully embellished. On Devil Got My Woman, the only other artist to feature twice, Skip James, may well have suggested not only Johnson's own "Hellhound On My Trail", but also the eerie, keening falsetto that Johnson substituted for House's gruff roar.

➲ We almost chose **The Slide Guitar Vol.1**, Columbia, 1990